The A to Z Field Guide to Canva

Published by TeacherGoals Publishing, LLC, Beech Grove, IN
www.teachergoals.com

Cover and Interior Design by Amanda Fox

Paperback ISBN: 978-1-959419-09-9

First Printing January 2023

Canva is a trademark of Canva Pty Ltd.

The Canva Classroom is an independent publication and has not been authorized, sponsored, or otherwise approved by Canva Pty Ltd.

Bulk purchases are great for your team of designers, teachers, or students.

TEACHERGOALS
PUBLISHING

Amanda Fox

The **A** to **Z**
FIELD GUIDE
to **Canva**

A User's Companion to Canva
Terms and Features

TEACHERGOALS
PUBLISHING

THE HITCHHIKER'S GUIDE FOR EDUCATORS SERIES

New Book from Amanda Fox

The Canva Classroom:
42+ Ultimate Answer to Templates that Rocket Student Engagement

With Canva taking the world by storm, designing templates for your business, classroom, or nonprofit is more accessible and easy than ever.

Unlock the power of design with this comprehensive glossary of over 300 terms and accompanying screenshots.

From basic design principles to advanced tools, this guide covers everything you need to know to master Canva and create stunning designs.

Whether you're a beginner or a seasoned designer, this glossary is the perfect companion to help you navigate the world of Canva and create professional-grade designs with ease.

Learn more about using Canva in the Classroom
https://teachergoals.com/books/educational-technology/

The Hitchhiker's Guide to Canva Series

THE HITCHHIKER'S GUIDE FOR EDUCATORS SERIES
THE CANVA SCHOOL
BY DANAE ACKER & DR. JOHN WICK

The Canva School picks up where The Canva Classroom finished. Reaching beyond the classroom this book will take a look at a systems approach to Canva implementation and how this tool can be leveraged to make leading, teaching, and learning easier and more efficient. Join forces with two incredible innovative thought leaders in the world of educational technology (Principal John Wick, and Digital Integration Specialist Danae Acker) as they guide you through the process of setting up a Canva ecosystem that works for small schools, large schools, private schools, and public schools. Learn from their experiences and journey in establishing Canva as one of the main components of school operations and vitality. You will gain access to useful templates, workflows, and resources that will make you wonder how you ever survived during the PC years (Prior to Canva).

THE HITCHHIKER'S GUIDE FOR EDUCATORS SERIES
THE CANVA CLASSROOM MATH EXPANSION PACK
BY HEATHER BROWN AND AMANDA FOX

This spin-off of the best-selling book, The Canva Classroom, focuses on sparking the love of math in students from kindergarten through high school. While most adults have experienced math anxiety at least at one point, this book will help to alleviate that anxiety for students and have them craving more math time! It goes beyond the standards commonly focused on in math and delves into the standards of mathematical practices which increase important life skills such as critical thinking and perseverance, and skills that every teacher dreams of instilling into their students.

THE HITCHHIKER'S GUIDE FOR EDUCATORS SERIES
THE CANVA CLASSROOM LITERACY EXPANSION PACK
BY KRISTINA HOLZWEISS

In our Literacy Expansion Pack Kristina covers Canva for Research, Reading, and Writing. It is filled with templates and ideas to support literacy for students of all ages and ability levels. Learn how to develop lessons, activities, and assessments that will increase student engagement and understanding of a variety of text formats. With Canva, your students will have an accessible "on-ramp" to creating projects such as book bentos, comics, and visual memoirs that combine multimedia elements including text, images, videos, and audio.

THE HITCHHIKER'S GUIDE FOR EDUCATORS SERIES
THE CANVA CLASSROOM SOCIAL STUDIES EXPANSION PACK
BY KATHERINE GOYETTE AND ADAM JUAREZ

Our fourth book in our Canva Series focuses on project-based design in the social studies classroom. In this book you will learn to use Canva to engage students as active consumers and creators of content in Social Studies, in concert with English Language Arts common core literacy standards. Motivate students to read, write, listen, and speak about Social Studies content via media rich templates made with today's learner in mind.

COURSES *by* TEACHERGOALS

REGISTER NOW!

Don't panic! Relax, because this course, based on *The Canva Classroom* book is designed as an educator's design guide to creating meaningful student tasks and projects using the Canva design platform. Each module is designed to help you fully leverage the Canva platform with the goal of embracing creativity, student voice, collaboration, critical thinking, and community. With over 8 hours of video enhanced instruction you are guaranteed to walk away a Canva pro!

01 Canva for Education Set Up

02 Designing For Inclusivity: UbD and UDL

03 Designing for Depth of Knowledge

04 Using Canva to Enhance Instruction

05 Canva Tips, Hacks, and Tricks

06 Canva App Integrations and App Smashing

07 Creating a Canva Brand Kit

08 Creating Learning Experiences in Canva

09 Feedback, Assessment, and Folders

10 Social Media and Community Building

PARTICIPANTS WILL:

- Learn how to set up a Canva Classroom and register for the Canva Education Dashboard.
- Explore pedagogical foundations such as Depth of Knowledge, Universal Design Framework, Backwards Design.
- Explore over 10 ways to app smash with Canva and be given examples.
- Complete learning tasks demonstrating understanding of Canva feature and functions.
- Experience the platform from a student perspective.
- Create a classroom, school, or district brand kit.
- Design an interactive lesson using Canva and its integrated functions.
- Learn how to organize folders, follow creators, and save elements.
- Explore multiple ways to provide feedback and assessment using Canva.
- Learn how to use Canva to engage socially and build a global PLN.
- Interact with other Canva Educators in the FB Group.

The **Canva Classroom Course:**

This course is the educators' design guide to creating meaningful student tasks and projects using the Canva design platform. Each module is designed to help you fully leverage the Canva platform with goal of embracing creativity, student voice, collaboration, critical thinking, and community. From pedagogical foundations, to design principles, and turn key templates, every design starts with the end in mind and is inclusive of all learners. Join now!

Get Canva Professional Development and Training From Our Experts

Amanda Fox

Adam Juarez

Katherine Goyette

Danae Acker

John Wick

Heather Brown

Kristina Holzweiss

Contact Us at:
https://teachergoals.com/pd/

Community Padlet Wall

Did you think of a term, feature, or tool not included in this field guide? Add the word, definition, and screenshots to our community Padlet wall for others to reference!

https://padlet.com/amandafox2/CanvaResource

Join Our Facebook Community

The Canva Classroom Facebook community is a community of Canva Using Educators that share tips, tricks, and templates to enhance education.

The A to Z Field Guide to Canva

A

B

C

D

E

F

G

H

I

J

K

L

M

N

O

P

Q

V

W

X

Y

Z

Why Canva?

Canva is a powerful, user-friendly online design platform that enables people to quickly and easily create stunning designs. It is available to users for free, but Canva also offers Canva Pro, Canva Enterprise, Canva for Education, Canva for Teams, and Canva Not-for-Profit. This extensive glossary of Canva design terms can help users quickly find descriptions of Canva features and better understand design concepts. This glossary was written as a supplement to the Hitchhiker's Guide for Educator's Canva series and courses to help new Canva adopters navigate the platform with ease.

Design is an important tool in communication, giving us the ability to express our ideas and stories in visually powerful and engaging ways. With the help of Canva, anyone can become a designer, building their own creative projects that are capable of having a major impact.

Whether you are a graphic designer, educator, small business owner, social media manager, or student this glossary is a great starting point to understanding all the features and tools that Canva offers.

If you are an educator or student be sure to check out TeacherGoals.com for Canva templates and use cases to maximize your Canva use in your classroom, school, or district.

 **A**

A4 Document:

An A4 document in Canva is a size template designed to match the international standard paper size of A4, which measures 21.0 x 29.7 cm (8.27 x 11.69 inches). It is a popular choice for creating documents such as flyers, posters, presentations, reports and brochures. Canva's A4 template is optimized for printing and offers a range of design options from simple grids to text and image layouts.

■■

Abstract

A type or style of element that can be found by searching Canva elements. You can find abstract lines, shapes, backgrounds, and art.

■■

Add Page

The "Add page" feature allows you to create a new page in a design. This can be useful if you are working on a multi-page design and want to add additional pages, or if you want to start a new design with multiple pages.

To add a page in Canva:

Open the design that you want to add a page to.
Click on the "Add page" button below your canvas or click the "Add Page" button (a plus sign in square) above the canvas in the right hand corner.

A new page will be added to the design.

When you add a new page in Canva, it will be blank and you can use the design tools and elements in Canva to create the layout and content for the page. You can also add existing designs or design elements from the "Uploads" tab in the left-hand toolbar to the new page.

The "Add page" feature in Canva is a useful tool for creating multi-page designs and for adding additional pages to existing designs. It is a particularly useful feature for designers who are working on projects such as brochures, reports, or presentations, which often require multiple pages.

Adjust

Adjust in Canva is a powerful suite of design tools that allows users to customize the look and feel of their designs. It can be used to edit photos, add text, change colors, crop and more. Adjust in Canva can also be used to create custom layouts, and resize designs for different platforms.

Aesthetic

A term used to describe the overall look and feel of a design, including the layout, colors, and style. Canva offers a wide range of aesthetic options for your designs

Alignment

A feature in Canva that allows you to align elements in your design to specific points, such as the center, left edge, or right edge.
■■

Align to Page

In Canva, the "Align to Page" feature allows you to align an object or group of objects to the edges or center of the page. To use this feature:

1. Select the object or objects that you want to align.
2. Click on the "Position" button in the top menu.
3. A submenu will appear, allowing you to choose how to align the objects. The options are:

- Align Left: Aligns the left edge of the objects with the left edge of the page.
- Align Center: Aligns the center of the objects with the center of the page.
- Align Right: Aligns the right edge of the objects with the right edge of the page.
- Align Top: Aligns the top edge of the objects with the top edge of the page.
- Align Middle: Aligns the middle of the objects with the middle of the page.
- Align Bottom: Aligns the bottom edge of the objects with the bottom edge of the page.

4. The selected objects will be aligned according to the chosen option.

You can also use the "Align to Selection" feature to align the objects to the edges or center of the selected objects.
■■

All Changes Saved

All changes saved in Canva are automatically saved to the cloud so that you can access them from any device. This means that you can pick up from where you left off, without having to worry about losing your work.
■■

Animated Text

In Canva, "animated text" refers to text that has movement or visual effects applied to it. Canva has a feature called "Animation" that allows you to add animation to your text and make it more dynamic and engaging.

To add animation to your text in Canva:
1. Select the text box that you want to animate.
2. Click on the "Animation" button in the top menu.
3. From the dropdown menu, select the animation that you want to apply.
4. The animation will be applied to the selected text box. You can adjust the duration and timing of the animation using the sliders that appear next to the animation name.

Canva offers a wide range of animations to choose from, including basic animations like "Fade In" and "Slide Up", as well as more complex animations like "Spin" and "Zoom". You can experiment with different animations to find the one that best suits your needs. Please note that animated text is not supported on all devices and browsers, and may not be visible to all viewers. You should test your design on different platforms to ensure that the animation is displayed correctly.

Animation

Animations are visual effects that add movement or motion to elements in your design. You can use animations to make your designs more dynamic and engaging, and to draw attention to specific elements or messages.

To add an animation to an element in Canva, select the element by clicking on it. Then, click on the "Animation" button in the top menu of the editor. This will open the "Animation" panel on the right side of the editor, where you can choose from a variety of animation options. You can select the type of animation that you want to use, such as a fade, slide, or bounce effect, and customize the timing and duration of the animation.

Once you have chosen and customized your animation, you can preview the animation by clicking on the "Play" button in the "Animation" panel. You can also use the "Animation" panel to change or remove the animation at any time.

Animations can be a useful way to add interest and movement to your designs, but it is important to use them sparingly and in a way that enhances the overall design rather than detracting from it.

API

The Canva API is a set of programming instructions and standards that allow developers to access and interact with the features and functionality of Canva's platform. The Canva API allows developers to create custom integrations and applications that can use Canva's design tools and resources to create and edit graphics.

Some examples of what can be done using the Canva API include creating custom tools for creating graphics, integrating Canva with other applications or platforms, or automating certain design tasks. The Canva API uses REST (Representational State Transfer) principles and returns data in JSON (JavaScript Object Notation) format.

To use the Canva API, developers must first apply for access and be approved by Canva. Once approved, developers can use the API to access Canva's design tools and resources, and to create custom integrations and applications. The Canva API documentation provides detailed instructions and examples for using the API and creating custom integrations.

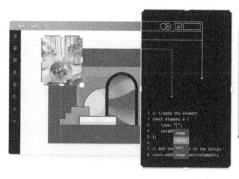

You can find more information on Canva API here:
https://www.canva.com/developers/

The A to Z Field Guide to Canva

Apps

Canva apps are applications that integrate within Canva and allow users to supercharge their designs, When you go to "all Canva apps: you are provided with a list of icons to apps that work within Canva. These apps are further broken into categories such as new, productivity, photo editing, design essentials, and share and publish. The apps are available for both iOS and Android devices.

Apps Continued

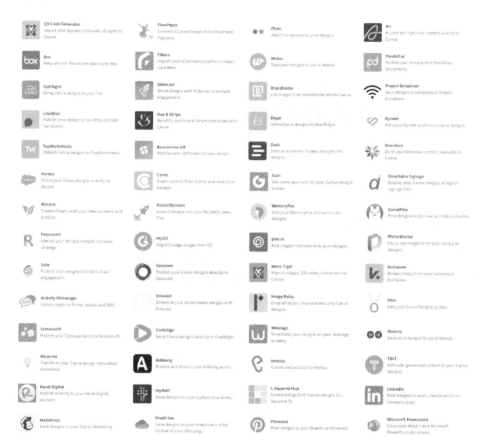

QR Code Generator — Import your dynamic QR codes straight to Canva!

Box — Keep all your files in one place with Box

OptiSigns — Bring Canva designs to your TVs

LoudDoc — Publish your design to LoudDoc and add narrations

TopWorksheets — Publish Canva designs on TopWorksheets.

Pardot — Share your Canva designs directly to Pardot

Wecora — Create designs with your Wecora items and publish.

Repurpost — Upload your designs straight into your strategy.

Sidle — Publish your designs to Sidle to track engagement

Activity Messenger — Canva images in forms, emails and SMS

Screensoft — Publish your Canva projects to Screensoft.

Wizer.me — Transform your Canva design into a Wizer worksheet

Revel Digital — Publish directly to your Revel Digital account

Mailchimp — Save designs to your files in Mailchimp

Slack — Share designs to your channels on Slack.

FlowPaper — Convert a Canva Design into a FlowPaper Flipbook.

Filkers — Import your eCommerce platform images via Filkers

Slidecast — Share designs with Slidecast to analyze engagement

Hue & Stripe — Beautify your Hue & Stripe Lookbooks with Canva

Beaconstac QR — Add Dynamic QR Codes to your design

Canto — Insert content from Canto and save your designs

RocketScreens — Export designs into your RocketScreens TVs.

my.G2 — Import badge images from G2

Sessions — Publish your Canva designs directly to Sessions

bobcaat — Schedule your social media designs with bobcaat

CodaSign — Send Canva designs directly to CodaSign.

AdAlong — Browse and import your AdAlong assets.

myWall — Save designs to your myWall data library.

OneDrive — Save designs to your OneDrive in a file format of your choosing.

Tumblr — Post designs on Tumblr

Flickr — Add Flickr photos to your designs

Wideo — Save your designs to use in Wideo

Brandfolder — Use images from Brandfolder within Canva

Edgar — Upload your designs to MeetEdgar

Dash — Drop your brand's images straight into designs

Gain — Get client approval for your Canva designs in Gain

MemoryFox — Add your MemoryFox stories to your designs

pixx.io — Add images from pixx.io to your designs.

Menu Tiger — Import images, QR codes, and more into Canva

Image Relay — Drop all of your brand assets into Canva designs.

Weezago — Broadcast your designs on your Weezago screens.

Intelisa — Create and publish to Intelisa

L Squared Hub — Create and publish Canva designs to L Squared TV

Pinterest — Post designs to your boards on Pinterest.

Twitter — Post designs on Twitter

Air — Access all of your Air content directly in Canva

PandaDoc — Publish your designs into PandaDoc documents.

Project Broadcast — Save designs to templates in Project Broadcast

Bynder — Add your Bynder assets into Canva designs

Starchive — All of your Starchive content, available in Canva.

Directable Signage — Display your Canva designs on digital signage TVs!

SocialPika — Post designs to your social media accounts

PhotoShelter — Easily use images from your Library in designs.

Kontainer — Access media from your company's Kontainer.

Xibo — Add your Canva Designs to Xibo

Moovly — Save your designs to use in Moovly

TINT — Add user generated content to your Canva designs.

LinkedIn — Post designs to your LinkedIn profile or company page

Microsoft Powerpoint — Download designs as a Microsoft PowerPoint document.

You can find a full list. here:
https://www.canva.com/you
r-apps/all-apps.

Arrange

A feature in Canva that allows you to adjust the order of elements in your design, such as by bringing an element to the front or sending it to the back.

••

Aspect Ratio

A term used to describe the relationship between the width and height of an image or design.

••

Audio

A feature in Canva that allows you to add audio to your designs, either by uploading an audio file or by linking to an audio file online.

••

Audio Only Recording

In Canva, the audio only recording feature allows you to record and add audio to your designs, such as narration or music. To use the audio only recording feature in Canva:

1. Open the design that you want to add audio to, and click on the "Audio" icon in the toolbar on the left.
2. Click the "Record audio" button to open the recording window.
3. Follow the prompts to grant Canva access to your microphone and begin recording your audio.
4. When you are finished recording, click the "Stop recording" button.

5. Preview your recording, and click the "Add to design" button to add the audio to your design.

Once the audio has been added to your design, you can use the audio tools in Canva to adjust the volume, trim the audio, or add effects. You can also use the audio only recording feature to add audio to an existing video by using the "Add audio" option in the video editing tool.

Autoplay

"Autoplay" is a feature in Canva that allows you to set a design to automatically play as a slideshow. This feature is useful for creating presentations or for showcasing designs on a website or other platform.

To use the "Autoplay" feature in Canva:
1. Open the design that you want to set to autoplay in the Canva editor.
2. Click on the "Share" button in the top right corner of the editor.
3. Go to "Present".
4. Click on the three dots in the bottom left corner of presentation view.
5. Select "Start Autoplay".

The "Autoplay" feature in Canva is a useful tool for automating presentation flow, or timing your slides. You can change the slide length in the settings by "editing timing". You can manually adjust the timing for each page or apply to all pages.

Auto-enhance

Auto Enhance is a feature in Canva that automatically adjusts the image, including brightness, contrast, saturation, and hue. It can help to improve the overall look and feel of your design, making it sharper and more vibrant.

Auto-resize

A feature in Canva that allows you to automatically resize a design to fit different dimensions or aspect ratios.

Autosave

A feature in Canva that automatically saves your design progress as you work, ensuring that you don't lose your work if you accidentally close the program or lose your internet connection.

B

Background

A feature in Canva that allows you to change the color or image behind your design elements.

Background Remover

A tool in Canva that allows you to remove the background from an image or graphic.

■■

BadTV

BadTV is an effect used in canvas and video processing that adds a grainy, distorted look to an image. It is commonly used to simulate an old TV or a cheap video camera recording. The effect is created by adding noise to the image, simulating the imperfections of an analog television display or video camera output.

■■

Banner

In Canva, a banner is an image that is typically used for advertising or promotion. It is typically placed at the top of a website or social media page. Banners are typically wider than they are tall and are used to draw attention to a particular message or product.

■■

Bar Chart

A bar chart in Canva is a type of graph that displays data using rectangular bars. It is used to compare values between different categories and can be used to measure changes over time. Each bar represents a category, with the length of the bar representing the value of the category. Bar charts are a useful way to visualize data and can be used to show trends, outliers, and comparisons.

Billings and Plans

In Canva, "Billings" refers to the billing and payment information for your Canva account. You can access your billing information by going to the "Billings" tab in the "Account Settings" section of your account.

The "Plans" section of the "Billings" tab allows you to view and manage your subscription to Canva. Canva offers several subscription plans, including a free plan and paid plans with additional features and resources.

If you are on a paid plan, the "Plans" section will show you information about your current subscription, such as the plan type, the billing cycle, and the payment method. You can use this section to update your payment information, change your plan, or cancel your subscription.

The "Billings" tab also includes a "History" section, which shows you a record of all of the charges and payments associated with your account. You can use this section to view past invoices and to manage your payment history.

Overall, the "Billings" and "Plans" sections of Canva allow you to manage your subscription and billing information for your Canva account.

■ ■

Blogs by Canva

Canva blogs are articles published by Canva, a graphic design platform. They provide helpful design tips, creative how-to guides, inspiring stories, and other information related to graphic design and visual marketing.

Access the Canva blog by going to : https://www.canva.com/learn/

Scan to access the Canva Blog

Blur

A tool in Canva that allows you to blur part of an image or graphic.

Book Cover

A type of pre-designed template in Canva that allows you to design book covers using free stock photography. You also have the option to design one from a blank design.

Border

A design element in Canva that consists of a line or outline around the perimeter of an element, such as a text box or image.

Brainstorm

A Brainstorm in Canva is an online brainstorming and collaboration tool that allows users to create, share and collaborate on visuals. It provides a variety of tools and features to help people come up with ideas and communicate their message in an organized and visually engaging way. It's great for team brainstorming, storyboarding, idea generation, and more.

■■■

Brand Management

Using Canva collaboratively, whether through teams, enterprise, or education, allows you to ensure your brand identity and guidelines are bring followed with fidelity. Brand management includes utilizing brand kit, brand templates, and brand control features for your team.
https://www.canva.com/for-teams/brand-management/

■■■

Brandkit

In Canva, a brand kit is a collection of assets and guidelines that define the look and feel of a brand, and helps you to apply your brand's visual identity to your designs. To create a brand kit in Canva, you can start by adding your brand's logo, color palette, typography, and imagery to your account. You can then use the brand kit to apply your brand's visual elements to your designs in a consistent and cohesive way. Canva allows you to save and manage multiple brand kits in your account, making it easy to switch between different brands or projects. You can also share your brand kits with others, such as team members or clients, to ensure that everyone is using the same brand assets and guidelines.

Brand Template

A brand template in Canva is a pre-designed set of graphics, colors, fonts, and other design elements that reflect the visual identity of a brand. It can be used as a starting point for creating marketing materials, such as social media posts, brochures, and business cards, in order to maintain consistency in the brand's visual appearance.

In Canva, you can create your own brand template by customizing the design elements to match your brand's style guidelines, or you can choose from a variety of pre-designed brand templates that are available in the Canva library. You can then save your brand template as a template, so that you can easily access and use it as a starting point for future design projects.

Brand templates can be a useful tool for businesses and organizations that want to ensure that all of their marketing materials have a consistent and professional look. They can also save time and effort by providing a set of predefined design elements that can be used as a foundation for new designs.

Brightness

A feature in Canva that allows you to adjust the overall lightness or darkness of an element, such as an image or graphic.

Bring Forward

"Bring Forward" is a feature in Canva that allows you to move an object or design element forward in the stacking order. This feature is useful for adjusting the layering of objects or design elements in a design.

To use the "Bring Forward" feature in Canva:
1. Open the design that you want to edit in the Canva editor.
2. Select the object or design element that you want to move forward.
3. Click on the "Position" button in the toolbar on the right.
4. Select the "Bring Forward" option from the drop-down menu.
5. The selected object or design element will be moved forward in the stacking order.

The "Bring Forward" feature in Canva is a useful tool for adjusting the layering of objects or design elements in a design.

Bring to Front

"Bring to Front" is a feature in Canva that allows you to move an object or design element to the front of the stacking order. This feature is useful for adjusting the layering of objects or design elements in a design.

To use the "Bring to Front" feature in Canva:
1. Open the design that you want to edit in the Canva editor.
2. Select the object or design element that you want to move to the front.
3. Click on the "Position" button in the toolbar on the right.
4. Select the "Bring to Front" option from the drop-down menu.
5. The selected object or design element will be moved to the front of the stacking order.

The "Bring to Front" feature in Canva is a useful tool for adjusting the layering of objects or design elements in a design.

■■

Brush

A tool in Canva found in that can be found in the "draw" app. You can use a pen, marker, glow pen, or highlighter brush. You can adjust the size, color, and transparency. Canva does not *yet* have any other brush or paint tools in the app.

■■

Bulk Create

In Canva, Bulk create allows you to save time creating multiple versions of the same design with. This is ideal when you're designing business cards, invitations, certificates, labels, or designs that require minimal text changes (e.g. names, dates, numbers, etc.).

Step 1: Accessing the Bulk Create tab
Go to the Bulk create tab to get started.

- Select a template or design you want to use for bulk creation.
- From the editor side panel, select Apps.
- Under More from Canva, select Bulk create.

Step 2: Importing data for Bulk Create

You can add the data to be used for Bulk create using different methods. You can enter data manually, upload images, or upload a

CSV file that includes the data. More on these below.

Entering data directly

If you prefer entering data manually, you can do it from the Bulk create tab.
1. From the Bulk create tab on the editor side panel, click Enter data.
2. Delete the sample data by clicking on Clear data.
3. Enter or paste the data into the table.
4. If you need to add more columns or rows, click on a table cell.
5. Click Accept to proceed.

Uploading images

You can also upload images. You can then connect these images to elements in the design covered in Step 3 below.
1. From the Bulk create tab on the editor side panel, click Enter data.
2. From the table, click Add data to add a new column.
3. Select Image.
Click the + icon on the cell to find the image or video you want to upload.

••

Bulk Edit

A feature in Canva that allows you to apply changes to multiple elements in your design at once, rather than making changes individually. You can change colors, text, and more by selecting a color or text box and changing the color or font. In the bottom of your left vertical panel tool bar you will see a "change all" feature.

Uploading a CSV file

Comma separated value (CSV) files are text-based files that allow data to be saved in a table format. CSV files are usually made using spreadsheet programs like Microsoft Excel, Google Sheets, or Numbers.

To save or convert a spreadsheet into a CSV file:
1. Open the spreadsheet with the data you want to use for Bulk create. If you don't have a spreadsheet yet, you can create one using the spreadsheet programs mentioned above.
2. Check that the data is in the correct order and in clearly labeled columns.
3. If you're using Google Sheets, click File and then Download. If you're using Microsoft Excel, click File and then Save As. If you're using Numbers, click File and then Export To....
4. Pick the .csv file option as the document type.

To upload a CSV file:
1. From the Bulk Create tab on the editor side panel, click Upload CSV.
2. Select the CSV file with the data for Bulk create.

See Step 3: Connecting elements below for the next steps.

Step 3: Connecting data to your elements

After uploading the data, the next step is connecting it to the elements on the design. For example, if you're creating a business card design, you need to connect the "First name" and "Last name" elements to the correct columns from the data table.

1. On the page of your design, right-click on the element you want to connect.
2. Click Assign data.
3. Select the data field you want to connect the element to.
4. If you'd like to attach an image, you need to add a frame element. You can add a frame from the Elements tab of the editor side panel.
5. Repeat from Step 2 until you've connected all columns. If your design has multiple pages, go to the page with the element you want to connect and repeat from Step 1.
6. Click Continue to proceed.

You can only connect one data field per element. For example, if your data table has "First name" and "Last name" as separate fields, you need to connect them to two elements: one element to connect "First name" and another to connect "Last name".

Step 4: Creating designs in bulk

The final step before bulk creation is to select which data to use.
1. Select the data you'd like to use. All data is selected by default. You can untick the data you don't want to use.
2. Click Generate. Once done, the pages created in bulk will open on a new tab.
3. Check if the pages are generated correctly. Adjust the elements as needed.

∎∎∎

Bulleted List

A feature in Canva that allows you to create a list of items with bullet points.

Button

A feature in Canva that allows you to add a button to your design that users can click on.

■■

C

Calendar

A pre-designed template in Canva that you can use to create a calendar. This could also refer to the social media calendar where you can schedule your social posts. For more information on this look at "schedule ."

■■

Canva Champions

The Canva Champions community is an application based affiliate program. Canva champions register as an affiliate and share a link with potential users to help grow the Canva community. Canva champions make money when people register for Canva Pro using their link. Find out more here: https://www.canva.com/affiliates/

■■

Canva Communities

Canva has various communities to support the use and dissemination of Canva. There are currently seven existing communities.

They each have their own Facebook group, and you must be accepted into the group to join. Check out the different communities here: https://www.canva.com/community/

Design Circle

The go-to space and community for all Canva users to discuss everything Canva, or anything design-related.

Canva Champions

Exists to empower, connect, and support Canva's Affiliates to grow their business and spread the word about Canva.

Canva Verified Experts

Canva Verified Experts are leaders and experts in their communities that get early access to Canva's product features.

Creators

Canva Creators allows creatives around the world to create, publish and earn from their designs on Canva.

Education Creators

Education Creators is a program within Canva that allows teachers to create, publish and earn from their educational templates on Canva.

Canva for Teachers

Canva Teachers communities are dedicated groups for educators, and helps to empower them to use Canva as a tool to educate.

Canva for Nonprofits

Canva Nonprofits community is a dedicated group for nonprofits, and helps to empower them to use Canva as a tool to communicate their mission and impact to the world.

Canva Creators

The Canva Creator program is an application-based design program where graphic designers, photographers, illustrators, typographers, and other creatives can apply to design assets for Canva to be shared within their platform. Canva Creators assets are added to the Canva marketplace and creators earn royalties based on their content's performance.

Canva currently has three types of creators: template creators, element creators, and education speciality creators. Once accepted as a Canva Creator all submissions or designs must pass a review process before they are made available in their platform.

Find out more here: https://www.canva.com/creators/

■■■

Canva Design School

Canva Design School is an online resource provided by Canva that offers design tutorials, tips, and inspiration to help users create professional-quality graphics. The Canva Design School includes a range of resources such as articles, videos, templates, and courses that cover a wide range of design topics and techniques.

Some of the topics covered by Canva Design School include design principles, color theory, typography, composition, and branding. The resources provided by Canva Design School are intended to help users learn more about design and improve their skills, regardless of their experience level or background.

You can access the Canva Design School by visiting the Canva website and clicking on the "Design School" link in the top menu. From there, you can browse through the available resources and choose the ones that are most relevant to your interests and needs. The Canva Design School is a useful resource for anyone who wants to learn more about design and improve their skills, and it is especially helpful for those who are new to Canva or design in general.

Find out more here: https://www.canva.com/designschool/

Canva Education

Canva Education is free to educators and includes access to the full range of Canva's design tools and features, as well as additional resources such as lesson plans, tutorials, and templates specifically designed for education. To join Canva Education, educators and students can sign up for a free Canva account and verify their status as an educator or student. Once enrolled in the program, they can access the full range of Canva Education resources and benefits.

Find out more here: https://www.canva.com/education/

••

Canva Enterprise

Canva Enterprise is a version of Canva that is designed for large organizations and enterprises. Canva Enterprise includes all of the features and resources of Canva Teams, as well as additional tools and support for enterprise-level organizations. Canva Enterprise is designed to help large organizations manage and scale their design needs, and includes features such as centralized asset management, advanced collaboration tools, and customizable workflows. Canva Enterprise also includes dedicated support from the Canva team, as well as additional security and privacy features.

••

Canva for Teams

Canva for Teams is a subscription-based collaboration platform that helps organizations design faster, smarter, and better. Teams can create marketing materials, social graphics, presentations, and more—all on the same platform. Very easy to use, Canva for Teams offers users access to a library of over 8 million photos, illustrations, templates, and fonts. It also offers seamless collaboration among team members, allowing them to comment on and edit projects in real time. This allows teams to create beautiful designs quickly and efficiently.

Find out more here: https://www.canva.com/for-teams/
■■■

Canva Free

The basic version of Canva is free to use and includes a wide range of templates, images, and design elements that users can access to create designs. Canva Free also includes basic design features such as text and shape tools, resizing and cropping tools, and the ability to upload and use their own images. While Canva Free is a powerful tool for creating designs, it does not include all of the features and resources that are available in Canva Pro, the paid version of the platform.

Find out more here: https://www.canva.com/free/
■■■

Canva Live

"Canva.live" is a feature in Canva that allows you to present a design as a live webinar or presentation. This feature is useful as a backchannel for hosting webinars, giving presentations, or conducting meetings with teams or clients. Participants can join with a simple 6 digit code, by going to canva.live. They can join the conversation, send reactions, comments, and questions as you present.

To use the "Canva.live" feature in Canva:

1. Open the design that you want to present in the Canva editor.
2. Click on "share" and click the "Present" button.
3. Select the "Canva.live" button in the bottom left hand corner of the screen (when you hover it will say "Interactive Q&A with Canva.Live."
4. Click on the "Start New Session" button to begin the Canva.Live session.
5. Share the 6 digit code with participants and have them put it in at Canva.Live.
6. Click on the "Stop" button in the Canva.Live column when you are ready to end the session.

The "Canva.live" feature is a useful tool for hosting webinars, giving presentations, or conducting meetings with teams or clients. It can be particularly useful for designers who want to share their work with a wider audience or who want to create video content for social media or other platforms.

■ ■

Canva Pro

Canva Pro is a paid version of Canva, a graphic design platform that allows users to create visual content for various purposes such as social media posts, presentations, and marketing materials. Canva Pro includes additional features and resources that are not available in the free version of Canva, such as access to premium templates, images, and design elements, the ability to upload and use custom fonts, and the ability to collaborate with team members. Canva Pro is designed to help users create professional-quality designs more efficiently and effectively.

Find out more here: https://www.canva.com/pro/

Canva Represents

The Canva Represents Fund is designed to seek out, support, and champion talented artists from underrepresented communities around the world

Find out more here: https://www.canva.com/canva-represents/

Canvas

The main work area in Canva where you create and edit your designs.

Canvassador

A Canvassador is a teacher leader who has applied and been accepted into the Canva Teacher Ambassador program. Canvassadors are invited to special networking events, host webinars, and are considered Canva experts who empower other teachers and students to reach their potential.

Find out more here: https://public.canva.site/teacher-cavassadors

Change All

In Canva, the "Change All" feature allows you to quickly apply a formatting change to multiple objects at once. For example, if you have a group of text boxes that all use the same font, you can use the "Change All" feature to change the font for all of the text boxes at once. You can also use this feature to change a color to a different color across the entire design or presentation.

To use the "Change All" feature:
1. Select the object, text, or color that you want to change.
2. Click on the "Change All" button that appears at the bottom of the left toolbar column.
3. Make your selections and click "Change All" to apply the changes.

Please note that the "Change All" feature only works with objects that have the same formatting. If you have a group of objects with different formatting, you will need to change them individually.

Charts

A tool in Canva that allows you to create various types of charts. The different types of charts you can make are below:

- Bar Chart
- Donut Chart
- Histogram chart
- Picture Graph
- Radial Progress
- Progress Ring
- Progress Dial
- Progress Bar
- Line Chart
- Scatterplot Chart
- Stacked Area Chart
- Pie Chart
- Stacked Bar Chart
- Row Chart
- Stacked Row Chart

Check List

A checklist in Canva is a template that allows users to create a list of items with checkboxes to keep track of activities or tasks. It can be used to help ensure important tasks are completed, manage a project's progress, or create a simple to-do list. It is a great way to visually track progress, break down tasks into manageable chunks, and ensure that tasks are completed in a timely manner.

A checklist is also a feature in the top toolbar. You can add bullet points or numbers by selecting text and clicking on the checklist icon.

Circle Crop

Circle Crop in Canva is a feature that allows users to crop photos or images into a circle so that it can be used as an avatar or profile picture. This feature can be accessed by searching for "frames: in elements and selecting the circle. You then drop your photo into the frame.

Learn more here: https://www.canva.com/features/circle-crop/

Class Details

In the education version of Canva, this is where you will be able to find and edit your classroom logo, homepage banner, name, and description.

Learn more about creating classes:
https://www.canva.com/help/create-and-customize-classes/

Class Schedule

You can create personalized class schedules in Canva starting from a plethora of pre-designed templates or from scratch. Simply search Canva for "class schedule" and pick a template that fits your style. Customize the template and then share digitally with students or you may choose to print it out.

Learn more here: https://www.canva.com/create/class-schedules/

••

Classwork

In the Canva for Education dashboard you will be able to find all your student work that has been submitted for feedback or review.

7G	7th Grade History Education • 8, 143	⌄	**Classwork**		New Activity
⌂ Home		All approvals ⌄			
⊞ Templates			Title	From	
▭ Projects					
Tools			Dominique vasquez Black histoy month	D Dominique Vas	
✉ Classwork					
🏛 Brand			black history month	K Kayliana Monja	
📅 Content Planner					
⠿ Discover apps			"if there is no struggle, there is no progress." [Black History Month Project - Aidan Webb]	A Aidan Webb	
🗢 Smartmockups					

••

CMYK

CMYK or 'Cyan, Magenta, Yellow, Key', is a color model that is used for print purposes. CMYK is a subtractive color, this means that we begin with white and end up with black. So, as we add more color, the result turns darker.

Collaborate

A feature in Canva that allows you to work with others on a design, such as by sharing access to a design or leaving comments and feedback.
●●

Collage Maker

A tool in Canva that allows you to create a layout featuring multiple images or graphics.

Find our more here: https://www.canva.com/create/photo-collages/
●●

Color Palette Generator

Canva Color Palette Generator is an online design tool that generates custom color palettes based on images, photos, and themes. It allows you to quickly and easily create unique and beautiful color combinations for your designs. It also enables users to save and share their color palettes with others.

Find out more here: https://www.canva.com/colors/color-palette-generator/
●●

Color Picker Tool

A tool in Canva that allows you to select a specific color from an image or graphic.

Color Wheel

The Canva Color Wheel is an interactive tool that allows users to mix their own custom colors and experiment with different shades, tints, and hues. You can select colors from the wheel by moving the pointer clockwise or counter-clockwise, or use the click and drag feature to adjust the balance of colors in the wheel. You can also adjust the brightness, saturation, and contrast of colors.

Learn more about color
theory here:
https://www.canva.com/colors/color-wheel/

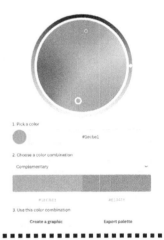

●●●

Comic Strip

Comic Strip in Canva is a feature that allows users to create customizable comic strips from their own photos, using text and design elements to create engaging and humorous stories.

Check out these templates: https://www.canva.com/comic-strips/templates/

Comments

In Canva, comments are a feature that allows users to leave feedback or notes on a design. Comments can be used to communicate with team members or clients about specific aspects of a design, or to ask for feedback or input.

To leave a comment in Canva, click on the "Comment" button in the toolbar at the top of the screen. This will open the comments panel on the right side of the screen, where you can type your comment and press "Post" to add it to the design. You can also use the comment tools to tag specific team members or to highlight a specific area of the design.

Comments can be a useful way to collaborate with team members or to get feedback on a design. When you leave a comment, it will be visible to other users who have access to the design, and they can respond to your comment or add their own comments. You can view all of the comments on a design by clicking on the "Comment" button in the toolbar, or by going to the "File" menu and selecting "Comments."

Concept Map

Canva has templates to create concept maps to quickly visualize, organize, and share your ideas.

Check out these Concept Map templates:
 https://www.canva.com/graphs/templates/concept-maps/

Content Planner

Canva Content Planner is a tool within Canva that helps users plan, schedule, and publish social media content. With Canva Content Planner, users can create a calendar of social media posts, organize their content by channel, and schedule posts to be published at a later time.

Canva Content Planner also includes features such as the ability to upload and store content, and to collaborate with team members on the content calendar. Canva Content Planner is designed to help users manage their social media content more efficiently and effectively, and to create a consistent and cohesive social media presence.

Find out how here: https://www.canva.com/help/content-planner/

Contrast

Contrast is the difference between two opposite elements such as light and dark, color, or size. It is used to draw attention to certain elements and create visual interest. Contrast can be used to make a design more visually appealing, as well as to make the message of the design stand out more.

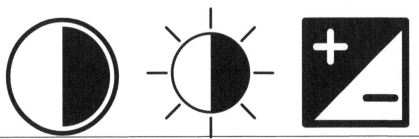

Copy

A feature in Canva that allows you to duplicate elements or designs, making it easier to create similar or related designs. You can also use the duplicate button

. . . .

Copy Style

In Canva, the "Copy style" feature allows you to copy the formatting and styling of one design element and apply it to another element. This can save you time and effort when you want to create multiple elements that have the same formatting and styling.

To use the "Copy style" feature in Canva, first select the element that you want to copy the style from. Then, click on the "Copy style" button in the toolbar at the top of the screen. This will copy the style of the element. Next, select the element that you want to apply the style to, and then click on the "Paste style" button in the toolbar. This will apply the copied style to the second element.

The "Copy style" feature can be used to copy and apply a wide range of formatting and styling options, including font, size, color, alignment, and more. It is a useful tool for creating designs with a consistent look and feel, and for quickly applying the same formatting and styling to multiple elements.

Copy to Clipboard

"Copy to clipboard" in Canva refers to the ability to copy text or an image to the clipboard, which is a temporary storage area in a computer's memory. Once something is copied to the clipboard, it can be pasted into another location or application using the paste command.

In Canva, the "Copy to clipboard" option is available for certain text and image elements. To use it, you will need to select the element that you want to copy and then double click with your mouse and select "Copy." This will copy the element to the clipboard, and you can then paste it into another location or application by using the paste command.

The "Copy to clipboard" feature can be useful if you want to reuse an element that you have created in Canva, or if you want to copy something from Canva and paste it into another application. It can save time and effort by allowing you to quickly and easily reuse elements that you have already created.

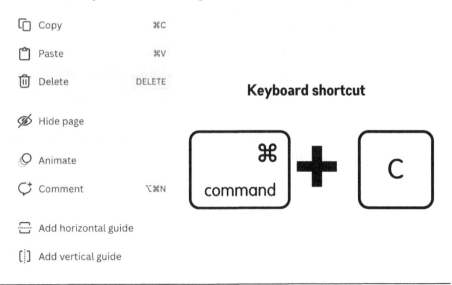

Creating a Class

Creating a class in Canva for Education is a way of organizing your designs into student groups. You can organize your designs by project or by subjects. You can also use classes to help manage the sharing of designs among members of a team. Once you join Canva for Education your first class will be created for you. You can change the class name by clicking on the "settings" button and "class details." To create a class in Canva, simply go to Home, then click on the "settings" button and "billings and classes" tab. From there, you can add new classes and name each one, as well as add members to each class.

You can find out everything you need to know about creating and changing class info here: https://www.canva.com/help/create-and-customize-classes

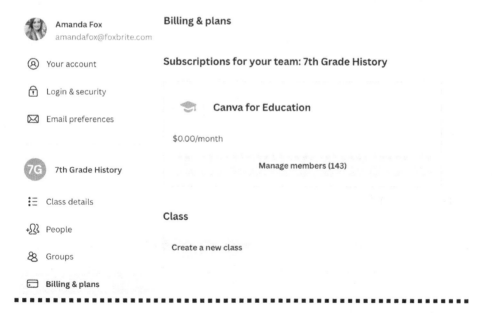

Crop

A feature in Canva that allows you to remove the outer edges of an element, such as an image or graphic, to focus on a specific area or aspect of the element.

■■

Curved Text Generator

A tool in Canva that allows you to bend or shape text or graphics into a curve.

Shape

Find out more here:
https://www.canva.com/features/curved-text/

ABCD | ᴀBCᴅ

None   Curve

■■

Custom Dimensions

A feature in Canva that allows you to create designs with specific dimensions, such as for specific print or web projects.

Find out more here: https://www.canva.com/help/design-from-scratch/

■■

Custom Font

A font that is not included with Canva by default, but can be added to your account and used in your designs by uploading it.

Learn about uploading fonts here: https://www.canva.com/help/upload-fonts/

Custom Size

Custom Size in Canva is a feature that allows you to create designs with your own unique dimensions. You can set a custom size for almost any type of document, from a blog header to a Facebook cover photo. With Custom Size, you can also select from a range of preset sizes for common documents on sites such as Facebook, Twitter and YouTube. Once you've chosen a size, Canva will automatically generate the correct dimensions and ensure that your design looks perfect

Dashboard

The Canva dashboard is the main control center for your Canva account, and provides an overview of your designs and activity on the platform. When you log in to your Canva account, the dashboard is the first page that you will see. The Canva dashboard includes a variety of tools and features that allow you to manage your designs and account settings, such as:

- A list of your recent designs, which allows you to quickly access and edit your designs.
- A search bar that allows you to find specific designs or templates.
- A menu of options that allows you to access different areas of the Canva platform, such as the design editor, the Canva library, and your account settings.

- A notification center that alerts you to new designs, comments, and other activity related to your account.
- A section that displays resources and tips for using Canva, such as tutorials and inspiration.

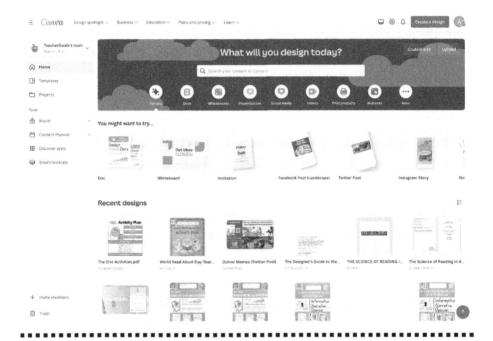

Delete

"Delete" is a feature in Canva that allows you to delete text, objects, or designs from your Canva account. This feature is useful for removing unnecessary or unwanted content from your Canva account.

To use the "Delete" feature in Canva:

1. Open the design or object that you want to delete in the Canva editor.
2. Select the text or object that you want to delete.
3. Press the "Delete" key on your keyboard to delete the selected content.

4. To delete a design, go to the "My Designs" tab in the Canva editor and select the design that you want to delete. Then, click on the "Delete" button in the top right corner of the design thumbnail.

The "Delete" feature in Canva is a useful tool for removing unnecessary or unwanted content from your Canva account. It can be particularly useful for designers who want to keep their Canva account organized and who want to remove content that they no longer need.

Design Circle

The Canva Design Circle is an open Facebook community for all Canva users to discuss Canva designs, hacks, tricks, and share templates. The purpose of the group is to share designs not only to inspire others, but also to receive feedback. Members can also learn new tips and tricks with our tutorials, as well as what's new in Canva. It is open to everyone.

Click here to join the Design Circle Group or scan the QR code:
https://www.facebook.com/groups/220885194946296

Design Essentials

In the app directory, design essentials are a sub category of apps that are available to edit your design.

You can find the design essential apps by going here: https://www.canva.com/your-apps/discover-content

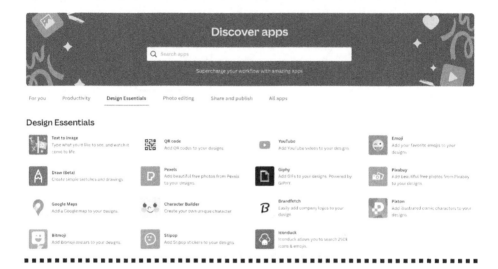

Desktop App

The Canva desktop app offers many of the same features as the web-based version of Canva, such as the ability to create and edit designs, access templates and elements from the Canva library, and collaborate with others on designs. However, the desktop app also offers some additional features and benefits, such as offline access and improved performance.To use the Canva desktop app, you will need to download and install the app on your computer. The Canva desktop app can be downloaded from the Canva website, or from the App Store or Google Play Store if you are using a Mac or Windows device. Once the app is installed, you can log in to your Canva account and access your designs and tools just as you would on the web.

Download for Mac:
https://www.canva.com/download/mac/
Download for Windows:
https://www.canva.com/download/windows/

■■■

Desktop Wallpaper

A template in Canva where you can create and customize a background wallpaper for your computer. There are over 12,000 templates that can be customized.

■■■

Diagram

A template type in Canva that allows you to create diagrams, flowcharts, and other types of visual representations of information. In Canva, a diagram is a visual representation of information or a process, such as a flowchart or an organizational chart. Diagrams can be created using Canva's diagram tool, which allows you to add shapes, lines, and text to create a visual representation of information or a process. You can use diagrams in Canva to create a wide range of visual aids, including flowcharts, mind maps, process diagrams, and more. Diagrams can be a helpful tool for explaining complex ideas or processes in a clear and concise way, and can be used in a variety of contexts, such as presentations, documents, and websites.

Find out more about the Canva Diagram Maker here: https://www.canva.com/graphs/diagrams/

Discover Apps

A button in the dashboard that allows you to search all the apps that are integrated into Canva.
You can search for apps that are integrated into Canva here: https://www.canva.com/your-apps/

Docs

Canva Docs are similar to Google docs and allows you to create internal documents or text heavy assets or writing assignments. You also can add style, color, movement, and visuals similar to presentations. Canva Docs has word processing features and you can connect external tools like Grammarly to edit your text.

A notable feature is the "Magic Write" capability that infuses artificial intelligence with your documents to craft text. See "Magic Write" for more information.

To learn more go here:
https://www.canva.com/docs/

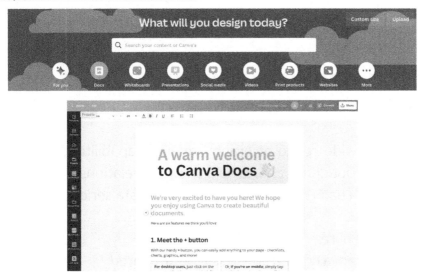

Docs to Decks

Canva Docs to Decks is a feature that allows you to convert your doc to a presentation in the click of a button.

Find out more here:
https://www.canva.com/help/docs-to-decks/

Docs to Decks
Plan your content and magically
turn it into a presentation

Dotted Line

A tool in Canva that allows you to create a line with dots instead of a solid line.

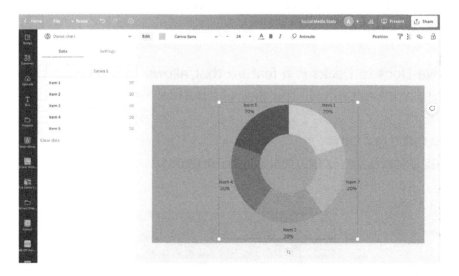

Donut Chart

Canva has a wide range of graph creation capabilities, including donut charts. Doughnut charts help show the relationships of parts to a whole with each ring corresponding to a data series.

Find out more here:
https://www.canva.com/graphs/doughnut-charts/

Draw Tool

A tool in Canva that allows you to draw freehand lines or shapes on your design. You can select colors, transparency, and size of your brushes in addition to pen, marker, highlighter, or glow pen. Once you have saved your drawing you can also resize it to fit your design.

Drop Shadow

A tool in Canva that allows you to add a shadow behind an image or graphic. You can find this by clicking on the element or image you wish to add a shadow to and clicking on "edit."

Duotone

A tool in Canva that allows you to edit photos with two colors. The duotone feature brings out the highlights with the brighter color and shadows with the darker color.

Try the feature here: https://www.canva.com/your-apps/AADrJDOkfRQ-duotone

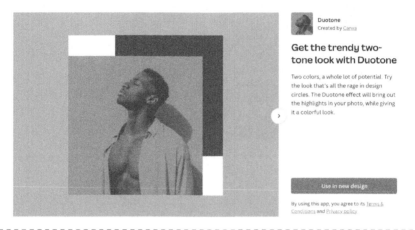

Duplicate

A feature in Canva that allows you to create a copy of an element in your design. You can copy elements, texts, pages, or entire designs.

Learn more here: https://www.canva.com/help/duplicate-designs/

E

Editing Element Timing In Video Presentations

A feature in Canva that allows you to edit the timing of animated texts and elements in a video presentation.

1. Create or open your video design.
2. Click on the element you want to edit.
3. To select multiple elements, hold **Shift** on your keyboard, and click to add other elements to the selection.
4. Right-click on the element then click on **Show timing**. The element timeline will appear on the video timeline below the editor.
5. Hover your mouse cursor over the element timeline's edge. Trim handles will appear.
6. Drag the handles to the left or right to adjust the timing and length of the element.

Learn more by going here: https://www.canva.com/help/edit-element-timing/

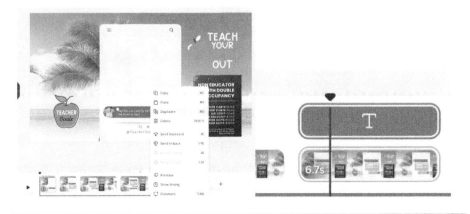

Editing Slide Timing

The "Editing Timing" feature in Canva allows you to edit or adjust the length of slides in a presentation up to 30 seconds. This is especially useful if you are using video or autoplay. To edit the timing of slides in Canva:

1. Open the design that you want to edit in the Canva editor.
2. Click on the "Edit Timing" button in the toolbar on the left.
3. Use the controls in the "EditTiming" window to adjust the timing of the slides.
4. Use the "Duration" slider to set the length of time that each slide will be displayed or manually input the number of seconds in the box.

The "Edit Timing" feature in Canva allows you to adjust the timing of slides in a design. This can be useful for creating timed presentations or when creating video content.

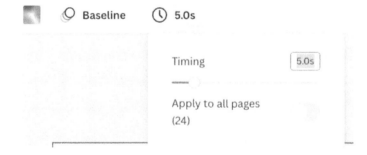

Edit Link

An edit link in Canva is a URL that allows someone to access and make changes to a Canva design. This can be useful if you want to collaborate with someone on a design, or if you want to allow someone else to make changes to a design that you have created.

To create an edit link in Canva, you will need to go to the "Share" tab in the top right corner of the editor and click on the "Link Shared Publicly" drop down. From there you will click on the "edit permissions' drop down and select "can edit." This will generate a unique URL that you can share with others to allow them to access and edit your design.

When someone clicks on an edit link, they will be able to access the design in their web browser and make changes to it using the Canva editor. They will also be able to download and print the design, unless you specifically disable these options.

Edit links can be a useful way to collaborate with others on a design, or to allow someone else to make changes to a design that you have created. They are also useful for sharing designs with clients or stakeholders who need to make changes or provide feedback on the design.

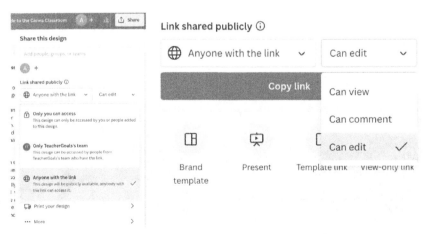

Education Creator

Education Creators is a program within Canva that allows teachers around the world to create, publish, and earn from their designs in Canva. Education Creators make templates that go through a review process to test their usability. Once they are approved they are available for other Canva users to copy, adapt, and customize for their needs.

Some of the benefits of the Canva Education Creator program include access to a dedicated support team, custom templates and resources, and professional development opportunities. The program is intended to help educators use Canva to create engaging and interactive learning materials, and to support student creativity and collaboration.

The program is open to educators at all levels, from primary school to university, and is available to teachers in a range of subjects and disciplines.

To apply go here: https://www.canva.com/education/education-creator/

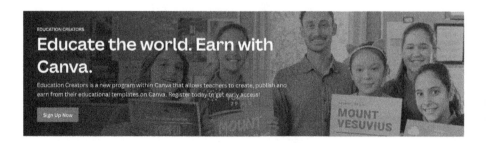

Effects (Elements and Text)

"Effects" are design features that allow you to apply visual changes to elements in your design, such as text, shapes, and images. Effects can be used to change the appearance of an element, add visual interest, or create a specific design effect.

Some examples of effects that are available in Canva include:

- Shadow: Adds a shadow effect to an element, which can create a sense of depth or make the element stand out from the background.
- Reflection: Adds a reflection effect to an element, which can create a sense of realism or add visual interest.
- Glow: Adds a glowing effect to an element, which can draw attention to the element or create a specific design effect.
- Blur: Blurs the edges of an element, which can create a sense of motion or distance.

To apply an effect to an element in Canva:
1. Select the element that you want to edit.
2. Click on the "Effects" tab in the design toolbar on the left.
3. Select the desired effect from the options available.
4. Use the controls in the "Properties" panel to adjust the settings for the effect.

More on image effects: https://www.canva.com/help/image-effects/
More on text effects: https://www.canva.com/help/text-effects/

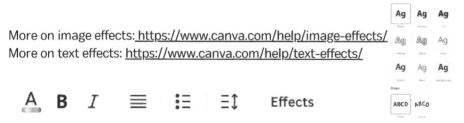

Element Animations

Element animations in Canva are effects that can be added to individual elements within a design to make them more dynamic and engaging. Element animations can include transitions, such as fading in or out, or more complex effects such as flying in or spinning.

To add an element animation to a design in Canva, first select the element that you want to animate. Then, click on the "Animate" button in the toolbar at the top of the screen. This will open the animations panel on the right side of the screen, where you can choose from a variety of animation options. You can add an animation to an element by selecting an animation from the list. You can then customize the animation settings, such as the duration and delay, to suit your needs in video presentations.

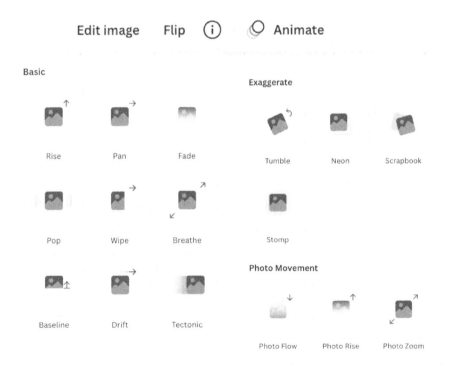

Elements

Elements are the building blocks of a design. They can include text, shapes, images, videos, audio, stickers, and other design elements that you use to create your design. Elements can be added to the canvas from the toolbar on the left side of the screen, or by dragging and dropping them onto the canvas from the elements tray. Once an element has been added to the canvas, you can customize it by using the options in the toolbar on the right side of the screen. For example, you can change the font, color, and size of text elements, or you can adjust the size and shape of shapes.

You can search for elements using the search bar and even use search filters to find the colors, animation style, and orientation you need.

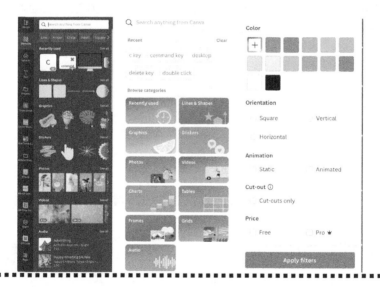

Embed a Canva Design

The embed feature in Canva allows you to embed a design that you have created in Canva on a website or blog. This means that the design will appear on the website or blog as a standalone element, rather than just a link to the design.

To use the embed feature in Canva, you will need to go to the "Share" tab in the top right corner of the editor and click on the "Embed" button. This will open a window with the embed code for your design. You can then copy the embed code and paste it into the HTML of your website or blog to embed the design.

The embed feature can be a useful tool for displaying your designs on your own website or blog, or for sharing them with others who want to include them on their own websites or blogs. It can also be a convenient way to showcase your designs to a wider audience.

Learn more here: https://www.canva.com/help/embed-designs/

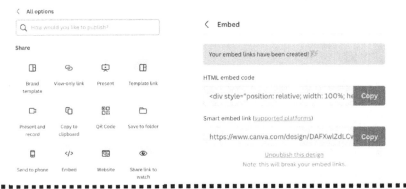

Embed Media Into Canva

In addition to embedding Canva designs in other places you can also embed media into Canva using the by using the "Embed" app.

Simply go to "apps" in the lefthand vertical toolbar and search for embeds.

Add video, music and online media to your designs.

Video: Music. Media. Embed it all with this handy app. Make your next presentation sing!

From there you can paste a link from another platform to embed it in the Canva design or select the specific media type you wish to add from the embed options.

Find out more:

https://www.canva.com/h
elp/embed-media/

Engagement

The Engagements tab is a feature in the Insights panel that lets you know how many times a person has interacted with your design.

For design link clicks, links are only tracked if they are clicked by design viewers and not while in the Canva editor.

Go to "Insights" for a more in depth look at Canva Analytics or read more here: https://www.canva.com/help/view-design-insights/

F

Face Retouch

A Canva tool that lets you automatically retouch and smooth out any blemishes, whiten teeth, and remove red eyes.

Try it now:
https://www.canva.com/your-apps/AAEdkl58rxk-face-retouch

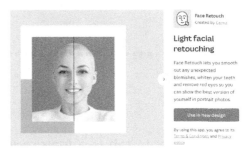

Filters

In Canva, "filters" are effects that you can apply to images or graphics to alter their appearance. Filters can be used to adjust the color, contrast, brightness, or other visual aspects of an image.
To use filters in Canva:

1. Select the image or graphic that you want to apply a filter to.
2. Click on the "Filter" button in the top menu.
3. From the dropdown menu, select the filter that you want to apply.
4. The filter will be applied to the selected image or graphic. You can adjust the strength of the filter using the slider that appears next to the filter name.

Canva offers a wide range of filters to choose from, including basic filters like "Brightness" and "Contrast", as well as more creative filters like "Vintage" and "Grayscale". You can experiment with different filters to find the one that best suits your needs.

Please note that filters are applied to the entire image or graphic, and cannot be applied to specific areas or elements within an image. If you want to apply a filter to only part of an image, you will need to crop the image or use another tool such as the "Adjustment" layer.

< Filters

Adjust	See all
Brightness	0
Contrast	0
Saturation	0

None   Epic   Festiv

Summer   Afterglow   Solar   Greyscale   Street

See controls

Selfie   Cali   The blues

Find and Replace Text

The "Find and Replace" feature allows you to search for specific text within your design and replace it with different text. This can be useful if you need to make changes to a large number of text elements at once, or if you want to quickly update your design with new information.

To use the "Find and Replace" feature in Canva, click on the text box you want to edit and click on "file." Select the "find and replace text" option from the drop down menu. This will open the "Find and Replace" window, where you can enter the text that you want to search for and the text that you want to use as a replacement.

You can also use the short cut keys "command" and the letter "f."

Once you have entered the search and replace text, click the "Replace All" button to update all of the matching text in your design. You can also use the "Find" and "Replace" buttons to update the text one element at a time.

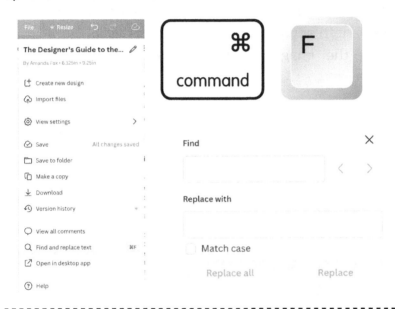

Flip

In Canva, the term "flip" refers to the process of reversing an image or graphic horizontally or vertically. Canva's flip tool allows you to flip an image or graphic horizontally, vertically, or both, which can be useful for creating mirrored or reversed versions of an image or for changing the orientation of an image to better fit a particular layout or design.

Folders

In Canva, a folder is a way to organize and group your designs and elements, such as templates, images, and graphics. You can use folders in Canva to keep your designs and elements organized and easy to access, and to share them with others. To create a folder in Canva:

1. Click on the "Folders" tab in the left menu of the Canva dashboard.
2. Click the "Create folder" button.
3. Enter a name for your folder and click the "Create" button.

Once your folder has been created, you can add designs and elements to the folder by dragging and dropping them into the folder from the dashboard or your design library. You can also add designs and elements to a folder by clicking the "Add to folder" button when you are creating or saving a design.

You can create as many folders as you need in Canva, and can access your folders by going to "projects" and clicking on the "Folders" tab in the dashboard.

Read more about folders here:
https://www.canva.com/help/create-folders/

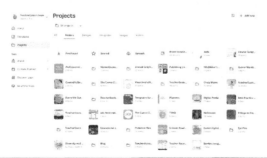

Font

In Canva, a font is a typeface that is used to display text in a design. Canva offers a wide range of fonts that you can use to add text to your designs, including both standard fonts and custom fonts. To use a font in Canva:

1. Open the design that you want to add text to, and click on the "Text" tool in the toolbar on the left.
2. Click on the canvas to place the text cursor, and then type the text that you want to add to the design.
3. Use the formatting options in the toolbar above the canvas to select a font for your text. You can choose from the standard fonts that are available in Canva, or you can upload your own custom fonts.
4. Use the other formatting options in the toolbar, such as the font size, color, and style, to customize the appearance of the text.

| Body Text | ∨ | − | 12 | + | A | B | I | ≡ | ⋮≡ | ≡↕ | Effects | ⋯ |

Learn more about uploading fonts here:
https://www.canva.com/help/upload-fonts/

Font Combinations

Font combinations refer to the specific pairing of two or more fonts that are used in a design. You can find pre-designed font combinations when you click on the "text" tab in the left hand vertical column of your design dashboard. When designing with text, it is important to consider the fonts that you use, as the right combination of fonts can help to create a cohesive and visually appealing design.

Frames

Find out more about frames here:
https://www.canva.com/help/using-frames/

Frames allow you to add or crop images and videos into a shape. In Canva you can find frames by going to the elements tab and searching for the word "frame." Frame is also a photo effect that allows you to add a frame around an image when you edit it.

Frames

Frames

 **G**

GIF

GIFs (short for "graphics interchange format") are image files that are used to display moving or animated images on the web. You can download designs from Canva as a GIF. GIFs compress a files size and do not include audio. These are great for animated tutorials, memes, and more. You can also add pre-existing GIFs by using the Giphy app integration, finding it in the vertical left toolbar under more apps, and adding them to your design.

  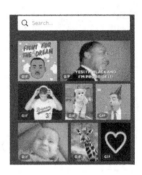

Google Classroom

Google Classroom is one of the more popular LMS integrations available in Canva for Education that allows users to connect Canva to create classes, publish assignments, and manage student teams.

To learn more about publishing assignments;
https://www.canva.com/help/publish-to-google-classroom/

Google Drive and Photos

Google Drive and Google Photos connects with Canva so you can bring your images directly into Canva in a streamlined workflow from within Canva.

Check out this tutorial to learn how to connect Google and Canva: https://www.iorad.com/player/1749395/Canva---How-to-Connect---Use-Google-Drive-Integration#trysteps-2

Graph Maker

Canva's graph maker allows users to create graphs or diagram quickly, turning data into an easy digestible visual viewers can understand. There are over 20 different types of graphs that you can create. Refer to each graph or chart's definition for more information.

Get started creating graphs here: https://www.canva.com/graphs/

The A to Z Field Guide to Canva

Types of Graphs

Area chart

An area chart shows quantities that change over time. A stacked area chart is helpful to show how different components contribute to the whole.

Bar graph

A bar graph is used to compare data across different categories. Each bar represents a category of data. The taller the bar, the bigger the number represented.

Comparison chart

A comparison chart is used to contrast between different options. It can be helpful for comparing different products or pricing models.

Donut chart

A donut chart is a kind of pie chart where the center has been removed. The area in the center can be used to display information.

Pie chart

A pie chart is a diagram showing the different components that make up a whole. It is a useful way to show fractions or percentages at a glance.

T-Chart

A T-chart is used for comparison. Two opposing perspectives or concepts are listed side by side.

Table

A table is a visual representation of data organized in rows and columns. It is a helpful tool for comparing facts and figures and making data-driven decisions.

Venn diagram

A venn diagram shows the similarities and differences between two sets of data. The overlapping area shows where the two sets have something in common.

Area chart

An area chart shows quantities that change over time. A stacked area chart is helpful to show how different components contribute to the whole.

Bar graph

A bar graph is used to compare data across different categories. Each bar represents a category of data. The taller the bar, the bigger the number represented.

Gantt chart

A Gantt chart is used to break a project down into tasks. It shows the estimated duration of a task, and the order of the tasks.

Line graph

A line graph is a useful way to document changes over time. It can be used to show changes in several different data sets in the one diagram.

Site map

A site map shows the different pages on a website and their relation to one another. It is a useful tool for SEO and for online navigation.

Strategy map

A strategy map helps to break down the strategy for a project or a business. It shows the goals or objectives and the proposed methods used to get there.

SWOT analysis

A SWOT analysis is a strategic planning technique. SWOT stands for Strengths, Weaknesses, Opportunities and Threats.

Venn diagram

A venn diagram shows the similarities and differences between two sets of data. The overlapping area shows where the two sets have something in common.

Work breakdown structure

A work breakdown structure breaks projects into tasks. It is a useful tool for project management.

Scatterplot

Scatterplots are used to represent a large number of data points. They are useful when there is a large amount of data, showing patterns in the chaos.

Block diagram

A block diagram is a simplified visual representation of a complex system or process using interconnected blocks, arrows, and lines. It is mostly used in engineering and the creation or design of hardware and software tools.

Bubble map

A bubble map is a brainstorming tool that lets you show the connections between related concepts or parts of a whole.

Concept map

A concept map is similar to a mind map. It is a tool for visualizing different ideas and showing the connections between them.

Cycle diagram

A cycle diagram shows the steps of a repeating or cyclical process. It helps display how one phase leads to the next.

Decision tree

A decision tree is a diagram that helps you to decide between different options by mapping out the possible consequences of each choice.

Diagrams

A diagram is a simplified illustration that represents structures and concepts. It shows how parts of a whole work together or how things relate to one another.

Ecomap

An ecomap is a way to show the different relationships in a person's life. It is commonly used as a tool in social work and nursing.

Family tree

A family tree is diagram showing the relationship between people in several generations of a family.

ER diagram

An entity relationship or ER diagram depicts the relationship between entities like people, objects, and concepts in a given database. Symbols like diamonds, ovals, and lines illustrate the interconnectedness and attributes of such entities.

Fishbone diagram

A fishbone diagram is a diagram that shows the relationship between cause and effect. It is a useful tool for identifying the causes of a problem.

Mind map

A mind map is used to show the different ideas associated with a particular concept. It is a useful tool for brainstorming.

Organization chart

An organization chart is a way of showing how a company is structured. It can be shown as a hierarchy with lines of reporting and different departments.

Gradient

A gradual change in color from one tone into another. Two common types of gradients are the linear gradient where each color sits on opposite sides of the frame, and a radial gradient where one color sits in the middle, and another at the edge. You can find different types of gradient elements by searching "gradients" in Canva's element search.

Check out these gradient templates:
https://www.canva.com/templates/s/gradient/

Graphic Organizer

Canva graphic organizers are professionally designed templates that can be used to create various visual representations of ideas, concepts, and thoughts. Examples include flow charts, mind maps, Venn diagrams, SWOT analyses, storyboards, timelines, and more. Graphic organizers are great tools for visualizing and communicating complex ideas in an orderly fashion.

Check out these Graphic Organizer Templates:
https://www.canva.com/graphic-organizers/templates/

Grids

Grids in Canva are help you position and align elements within your design. Grids are divided into a series of horizontal and vertical lines or frames, creating a series of intersecting points. You can use the grids as a reference to help you position elements accurately and ensure that they are aligned with each other.

Learn more about using grids:
https://www.canva.com/help/using-grids/

Group   Position

Group Elements

A group is a collection of design elements that are combined and treated as a single unit. Groups in Canva allow you to organize and manage multiple elements in your design, and to make changes to multiple elements at the same time. To create a group in Canva:

1. Select the design elements that you want to include in the group. You can select elements by clicking on them individually, or by dragging a selection box around multiple elements.
2. Click the "Group" button in the toolbar above the canvas.
3. The selected elements will be combined into a single group.

See "ungroup to learn how to ungroup items.

Read more on Grouping:
https://www.canva.com/help/layer-group-align/

Groups

An organizational feature that helps you work and share resources better within your team or class by creating groups.

1. On the top corner of the homepage, click the gear icon to go to Account settings.
2. From the side menu, click Groups.
3. On the upper corner of the page, click Create a group.
4. Give your group a name.
5. On the Administrator or Member field (Teacher or Student field for Canva for Education), enter the email addresses or names of the people that you want to add to the group.
6. Click Create group to finish.

Learn more here:
https://www.canva.com/help/groups/

Guides

Guides are a tool in Canva that to help with alignment proper alignment.

To see rulers and guides you click on file in the top tool bar and select "view settings" and "show rulers and guides." Your rulers will pop up all around the document to help with alignment.

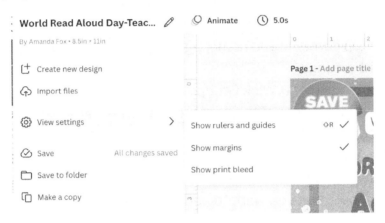

Read more here: https://www.canva.com/help/margins-bleed-crop-marks/

Halftone

Halftone is and effect in which the various tones of gray or color are produced by variously sized dots of ink. In Canva the effect is achieved by using the "screen" filter. See "screen."

Handwriting

Using the draw tool users can hand handwriting and signatures to their documents and designs.

▪▪▪

Headings and Subheadings

A heading is a main title, and a subheading is the text below that adds information about the headline, or that sets apart sections of an article or book. In Canva you can create brand kits that have font pairings of different fonts for your headings and subheadings.

Check out this Canva article on font pairings: https://www.canva.com/learn/the-ultimate-guide-to-font-pairing/

▪▪▪

Help

In Canva, the "Help" feature provides access to a variety of resources and support options to help you use Canva effectively and troubleshoot any issues that you might encounter. You can access the "Help" feature by clicking on the "Help" button in the top menu of the editor or by clicking on the question mark in the bottom left corner of your editor screen.

From the "Help" menu, you can access a range of resources such as the Canva Help Center, which contains articles and tutorials on how to use Canva and its features. You can also use the "Help" menu to access the Canva community forum, where you can ask

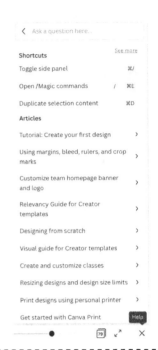

questions and get help from other Canva users, or to contact the Canva support team for assistance with specific issues or questions.

The "Help" feature is a useful resource for getting help with Canva and learning more about how to use its features and tools. It can be especially helpful if you are new to Canva or if you are experiencing any issues or problems with the app.

Hex-Code

In Canva, a hexcode is a six-digit code that represents a specific color. Hexcodes are commonly used in web design and digital graphics to specify colors. In Canva, you can use hexcodes to select a specific color for text, graphics, or other design elements.

To use a hexcode in Canva, you can enter the code directly into the color picker or color palette tool. Hexcodes are made up of a combination of letters and numbers, and each digit or letter represents a specific value of red, green, or blue (RGB) in the color. For example, the hexcode "FFFFFF" represents white, while "000000" represents black.

Hide Live Edits

The "Hide Live Edits" feature allows you to hide live collaborations on a presentation as you present it. The opposite "Show live Edits" allows your presentation to reflect edits being made in real time as you present. Showing Live Edits is beneficial if you are presenting and have share the edit link to the presentation with your audience and expect them to collaborate or add information to your presentation.

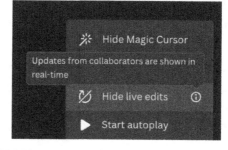

• •

Highlight

Canva does not have a traditional text highlighter tool. Instead you have to play with text effects. To highlight text you will select the text you want to be highlighted and then click on "effects." Next choose the "background style" and choose the color you want to highlight with.

Pro-tip: You will need to create a separate text box for isolated text you want highlighted or it will apply the background effect to the whole text box.

Histogram Chart

A histogram chart is a type of bar graph that displays the frequency of occurrence of a particular set of data. It is used to illustrate the distribution of a numerical variable and is typically used for descriptive purposes, such as showing the average height of a group of people or the average number of days in a month that it rains. The horizontal axis of a histogram chart shows the range of values and the vertical axis indicates the count or frequency of occurrence.

Read more on Histograms:
https://www.canva.com/graphs/histograms/

Make a Histogram

Home

Home is the dashboard view of Canva when you login.

Horizontal Flip

Horizontal flip is an option in your toolbar to flip an image or graphic horizontally.

Hue

A term used to describe the color of an image or graphic. Canva's color wheel allows you to adjust the hue of an image or graphic.

Icon

Canva offers free icons in their platform that can be accessed by searching "icons" in elements or through the app offerings. Iconduck and IconScout are two great tools to find icons for your designs.

Read more:
https://www.canva.
com/features/free-
icons/

Illustration

A visual representation of an idea or concept, typically created using lines, shapes, and other graphic elements. Canva has a library of illustrations that you can use in your designs. You can even search by styles such as "watercolor" and "digital art."

Image

A visual element in Canva that you can use in your designs, such as a photograph, icon, or graphic. Images can be searched or uploaded to Canva for use in a design.

■ ■

Image Converter

You can convert images in Canva into any image format, like magic. You can use the image converter to turn your photos into a format suited to your platform or project (JPEGS, SVGS, PNGs, GIFS), without worrying about losing image quality.

Read more:
https://www.canva.com/features/image-converter/

■ ■

Import

A feature in Canva that allows you to bring in elements from other sources, such as images or graphics from your computer or from other design tools.

■ ■

Info

When you are in a design you can find the info button by clicking on an element. In the top toolbar an i inside a circle will appear. If you click on it will give you more information on the element such as its name and keywords or metadata associated with it.

Infographic Charts

A visual element in Canva that you can use in your designs, such as a photograph, icon, or graphic. Images can be searched or uploaded to Canva for use in a design.

Read more:
https://www.canva.com/infographics/

■■

Insights

In Canva, "Insights" is a feature that provides analytics and information about the performance of your designs. It is available to Canva Pro, Canva for Education and Enterprise users, and it allows you to track the engagement and reach of your designs across social media and other platforms.

To access the "Insights" feature in Canva, go to the "Insights" tab in the top menu of the Canva editor. From there, you can view a variety of data and metrics related to your designs, such as the number of views and shares on social media, the engagement rate, and the demographics of your audience.

The "Insights" feature can be useful for understanding how your designs are being received and used, and for identifying areas where you can improve your design strategy. It can also help you to track the effectiveness of your marketing efforts and make data-driven decisions about your design content.

On the next page you can see screenshots from my insights on a design.

The A to Z Field Guide to Canva

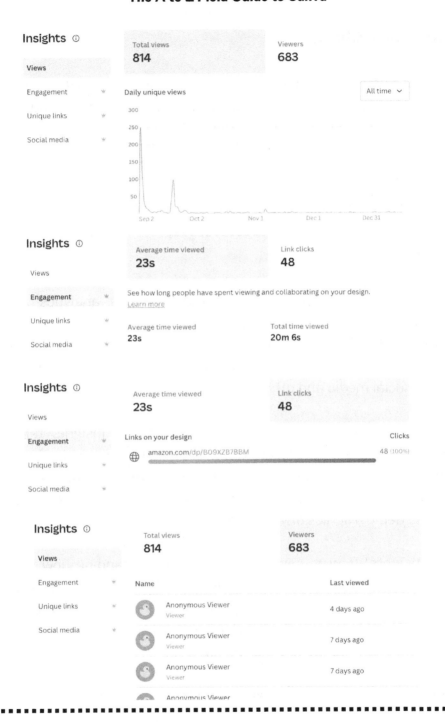

Insights ⓘ

Views

Engagement

Unique links

Social media

Total views
814

Viewers
683

Daily unique views

All time ⌄

300
250
200
150
100
50

Sep 2   Oct 2   Nov 1   Dec 1   Dec 31

Insights ⓘ

Views

Engagement

Unique links

Social media

Average time viewed
23s

Link clicks
48

See how long people have spent viewing and collaborating on your design.
Learn more

Average time viewed
23s

Total time viewed
20m 6s

Insights ⓘ

Views

Engagement

Unique links

Social media

Average time viewed
23s

Link clicks
48

Links on your design   Clicks

🌐   amazon.com/dp/B09XZB7BBM   48 (100%)

Insights ⓘ

Views

Engagement

Unique links

Social media

Total views
814

Viewers
683

Name   Last viewed

Anonymous Viewer
Viewer   4 days ago

Anonymous Viewer
Viewer   7 days ago

Anonymous Viewer
Viewer   7 days ago

Anonymous Viewer

Invite Members/Invite Students/Invite to Team

In Canva, the "Invite people" feature allows you to invite other users to join your team or collaborate on a design. With the "Invite people" feature, you can invite other Canva users to join your team, or you can invite people who are not yet Canva users to join by sending them an email invitation.

To invite people to join your Canva team:
1. Go to the "Team" tab in the left-hand toolbar.
2. Click on the "Invite people" button.
3. Enter the email addresses of the people that you want to invite to your team.
4. Click the "Send invites" button to send the invitations.

To invite people to collaborate on a design:
1. Open the design that you want to invite people to collaborate on.
2. Click on the "Collaborate" button in the toolbar above the canvas.
3. Enter the email addresses of the people that you want to invite to collaborate on the design.
4. Click the "Invite" button to send the invitations.

The "Invite people" feature in Canva is a useful tool for collaborating with others on designs and for building and managing a team in Canva. It allows you to easily invite other users to join your team or collaborate on a design, and makes it easy to work together on projects in Canva

Read more:
https://www.canva.com/help/manage-members/

Italic A **B** *I* U̲ aA

A typeface style that slants the letters to the right, typically used for emphasis or to indicate a foreign word. Canva allows you to apply the italic style to text in your designs.

J

JPG/JPEG

JPEG (Joint Photographic Experts Group) is a popular image file format that is widely used for storing and sharing digital images. JPEG is a lossy format, which means that it uses compression to reduce the file size of an image, but also results in some loss of quality.

JPEG is a good choice for storing and sharing photographs and other images that have a wide range of colors and gradients, as it is able to maintain a high level of detail and color quality while still keeping the file size relatively small. It is particularly well-suited for use on the web, as it can be easily displayed in web browsers and uploaded and downloaded quickly.

JPEG images are often identified by their file extension, which is typically ".jpg" or ".jpeg."

You can download designs from Canva as JPGS.

Justify

To justify text in Canva, you can select the text box and click on the "Justify" button in the toolbar above the canvas. This will align the text with both the left and right margins, and adjust the spacing between words and letters to create a straight edge on both sides of the text.

To use the "Justify" feature in Canva:
1. Select the text box that you want to align.
2. Click on the "Justify" button in the toolbar above the canvas.
3. Choose the desired alignment option from the drop-down menu.

The "Justify" feature in Canva is a useful tool for aligning text in your designs and ensuring that it looks visually balanced and well-organized. It is particularly useful for designers who are working on projects such as newsletters, reports, or other documents that require text to be aligned with specific margins or justified.

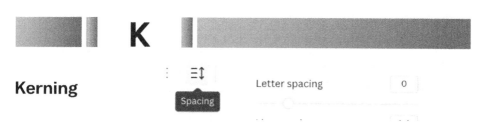

K

Kerning

The horizontal spacing between two consecutive characters; adjusting the kerning creates the appearance of uniformity and reduces gaps of white space between certain letter combinations. Kerning can be achieved or altered in Canva by selecting "spacing" in your top toolbar and using the line slider to adjust letter spacing.

Keyboard Shortcuts

A keyboard shortcut is a combination of keys that, when pressed at the same time, can be used to perform a specific action or command in a software or operating system. A list of keyboard shortcuts available in Canva are on the next page.

Copy: Cmd/Ctrl + C
Paste: Cmd/Ctrl + V
Quick Copy: Alt/Option + Drag
Add a text box: T key
Bold text: Cmd/ctrl + B
Italicized text: Cmd/ctrl + I
Underline text: Cmd/Ctrl + U
Increase font size: Cmd/Ctrl + Shift + >
Decrease font size: Cmd/Ctrl + Shift + <
Copy text style: Cmd/Ctrl + Option/Alt + C
Paste text style: Cmd/Ctrl + Option/Alt + V
Convert text to uppercase: Cmd/ctrl + Shift + K
Align text to the left: Cmd/ctrl + shift + L
Align text to the right: Cmd/ctrl + shift + R
Align text in the center: Cmd/ctrl + shift + C
Group elements: Cmd/Ctrl + G
Ungroup elements: Cmd/Ctrl + Shift + G
Duplicate elements: Cmd/ctrl + D
Select all elements: Cmd/ctrl + A
Deselect element: ESC key
Delete element: Delete key
Send elements backward: Cmd/ctrl + [
Send elements forward: Cmd/ctrl +]
Send elements to back: Cmd/ctrl +Option/Alt + [

Send elements to front: Cmd/ctrl + Option/Alt +]
Add a line to your template: L key
Add a rectangle to your template: R key
Add a circle to your template: C key
Constrain proportions while resizing: Shift + Drag Corners
Scale element relative to it's center point: Alt + Drag Side Handles
Zoom in on your template: Cmd/ctrl + "+"
Zoom out of your template: Cmd/ctrl + "-"
Zoom 100%: Cmd/ctrl + 0
Zoom to fit: Cmd/ctrl + Option/Alt + 0
Undo an action: Cmd/ctrl + Z
Redo an action: Cmd/ctrl + Shift + Z
Add a new page: Cmd/Ctrl + Return key
Delete empty page: Cmd/Ctrl + Delete key
Add a comment: Cmd/Ctrl + Option/Alt + M
Select multiple elements: Shift + Click

L

Label Maker

You can design professional-quality labels with Canva's free online label maker. There are tons of templates to choose from, or you can design from a blank canvas.

Learn more: https://www.canva.com/create/labels/

Landscape

Landscape orientation is a page orientation that is wider than it is tall, where the width is greater than the height. It is used for large displays, such as posters, and for landscape photographs. You can change the orientation or size of a design by going to resize and putting in the custom dimensions you want to resize to.

Layer

A feature in Canva that allows you to arrange elements in your design in layers, with each layer occupying a different position in the stack. You can change the layer of an element or text by clicking on position in your top toolbar.

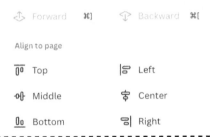

Letter Mosaic

Letter Mosaic is a image/element feature that lets you add a futuristic feel when applied. Think of the Matrix.

Letter Spacing

"Letter spacing" is a design feature that allows you to adjust the amount of space between characters in a text box. You can use letter spacing to make text more legible, to create visual balance in a design, or to achieve a specific design effect.

Line

A design element in Canva that consists of a straight path connecting two points. Canva allows you to add lines to your designs and customize their appearance.

Line Graph/Chart

A line chart is a type of graphical representation in which data points are connected with a line. The line is used to show a trend or relationship between two or more data sets. Line charts are often used to show changes in data over a period of time and are especially useful for trends that show an overall increase or decrease. They are also helpful for identifying patterns in data and comparing data sets.

Read more here:
https://www.canva.com/gra
phs/line-graphs/

Line Spacing

A feature in Canva that allows you to adjust the space between lines of text in your design.

▪▪▪

Link

A feature in Canva that allows you to add a hyperlink to your design, which can be clicked to open a web page or other online content.

▪▪▪

Liquify

Liquify is a photo filter app in Canva that creates a liquidy, drippy, under water effect to photos.

Liquify

▪▪▪

LMS Integrations

LMS (Learning Management System) integrations in Canva allow you to connect your Canva account to your LMS platform, enabling you to access and use Canva directly with your LMS. This can be useful for creating and sharing learning materials or course content, or for using Canva as part of your e-learning or instructional design workflow.

To use LMS integrations in Canva, you must first have an LMS platform that is compatible with Canva. Currently, Canva supports integrations with several popular LMS platforms, including Google Classroom, Schoology, Blackboard, Canvas, D2L, and Moodle.

To set up an LMS integration in Canva, go to the "Account Settings" menu in your Canva account and select the "Integrations" tab. From there, you can follow the prompts to connect your Canva account to your LMS platform. Once the integration is set up, you will be able to access and use Canva directly from within your LMS, and you can share your Canva designs with your students or learners as needed.

LMS integrations can be a useful way to streamline your e-learning workflow and make it easier to create and share learning materials with your students. They can also help to ensure that your learning content is consistent and professional-looking, as you can use Canva's design tools and resources to create high-quality materials

Read more here: https://www.canva.com/education/lms-integrations/

Lock

The "Lock" feature allows you to prevent a design element from being accidentally moved, resized, or edited. When an element is locked, it will stay in place and you will not be able to make any changes to it until it is unlocked.

To lock an element in Canva, click on the element to select it, and then click on the "Lock" button in the toolbar at the top of the screen. This will lock the element in place and prevent it from being moved or edited. To unlock the element, click on the "Lock" button again.

The lock feature can be useful when you are working on a design with multiple elements and you want to make sure that certain elements stay in place. It can also be helpful when you are working with a team and you want to prevent other team members from accidentally making changes to certain elements of the design.

Login

A feature in Canva that allows you to access your account and start creating designs. You must create an account with Canva in order to access the platform. You can login with Google, Facebook, Email, and more.

Log in or sign up in seconds

Use your email or another service to continue with Canva (it's free)!

G   Continue with Google

Continue with Facebook

✉   Continue with email

Continue another way

By continuing, you agree to Canva's Terms of Use. Read our Privacy Policy.

Sign up with your work email

M

Magazine Cover

A popular template available in Canva that allows you to select from pre-designed magazine covers to help your publication stand out from the crowd.

View templates here: https://www.canva.com/magazine-covers/templates/

■■

Magic Resize

A feature in Canva that allows you to quickly resize an element to fit a specific size or aspect ratio. You can change a Instagram design to a Twitter post in the click of a button. You may have to adjust your design slightly to fit the new canvas size.

■■

Magic Shortcut

A feature in Canva that allows you to activate fun animations by pressing the following shortcuts on your keyboard:

Magic Shortcut Keys

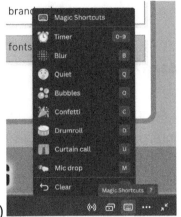

- Letter B to blur the current slide
- Letter C for confetti rain
- Letter D for a drumroll animation
- Letter M for a mic drop animation
- Letter O for floating bubbles
- Letter Q for quiet
- Letter U for a curtain call animation
- Any number (0-9) for a timer

(1 for one minute, 2 for two minutes, etc.)

Magic Write

Magic Write is a powerful AI-driven writing aid that makes text creation simple and easy for everyone. Whether it's for social media posts, business plans, websites, blogs, poems, journals, creative writing, or something else entirely, this tool can generate sentences, paragraphs, lists, and outlines based on the content you enter. It is currently only available in Canva Docs.

Read more here:
https://www.canva.com/help/magic-write/

WRITE A PARAGRAPH ON MAGIC WRITE

Magic Write is a powerful tool that can help anyone become a better writer. It can help you stay organized, and provide you with the necessary tools to create beautiful, organized, and concise writing. It can also help you think more deeply and creatively about the topics you are writing about, allowing you to create more meaningful and interesting pieces. Magic write can also help you develop a better understanding of grammar, spelling, and punctuation, which is a great way to improve your writing skills. It also has a range of features, such as a spell checker, thesaurus, and a variety of templates, which can be used to help you create an even better writing experience. Magic write is an invaluable tool for anyone who wishes to become a better writer.

Generated with AI using canva.com/magic-write
This technology is new and improving, please check the accuracy before sharing

Margins

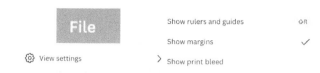

In Canva, margins refer to the empty space around the edges of a design. The margins of a design can be adjusted by changing the size of the canvas or the size of the elements within the design. Adjusting the margins of a design can help to balance the layout and ensure that the design looks visually appealing. In Canva, you can adjust the margins of a design by changing the size of the canvas or by using the alignment tools to position the elements within the design.

Read more here:
https://www.canva.com/help/margins-bleed-crop-marks/

Meme Maker

A feature in Canva that allows you to create memes with their drag-and-drop editor. There are hundreds of free templates you can use to create funny content to share on your socials.

Learn more here:
https://www.canva.com/create/memes/

Mind Map

Canva offers close to 1,000 mind templates for brainstorming and planning. Mind maps are diagrams used to visually organize information. They usually consist of central concept surrounded by related ideas and details branching off from the center.

Mind maps can be used to brainstorm, outline ideas, take notes, and even create presentations. Mind maps are a great way to organize and retain large volumes of information, as they make use of color and visuals to represent concepts..

Read more here:
https://www.canva.com/mind-maps/templates/
▪▪▪

Mirror Image

You can achieve a mirror effect of images by using the "flip" tool in the top toolbar. See "flip" for more information.
▪▪▪

Mobile Video

Canva has a ton of templates for mobile video creation. Most mobile videos are in vertical format and can be shared as reels on Instagram, Facebook, and TikTok. Present your video content in style with our free, customizable mobile phone video templates.

Learn more here:
https://www.canva.com/mobile-videos/templates/

MP4

MP4 is an acronym for MPEG-4 Part 14, and the file format was created by the Moving Picture Experts Group (MPEG) as a standardized way to store audio, video, and other data. MP4 files are widely used because they are compatible with many different devices and software programs, and they can be played on a wide range of devices including smartphones, tablets, and personal computers. You can download designs with animations or videos as MP4 by going to the top menu above your canvas and selecting "download" and then "MP4."

N

Not For Profit

Canva provides Not-For-Profit companies and organizations access for free. Read more here: https://www.canva.com/canva-for-nonprofits/

Notes

The notes feature allows you to add comments or annotations to your design by clicking on the "Notes" button in the bottom left hand tool bar. Notes can be useful for communicating with team members or clients about specific elements or details in your design, or for leaving yourself reminders or notes about changes that need to be made. Notes will save for each page or slide in design.

You can also use the "Notes" panel to view any notes that have been added to your design.
Notes are only visible to you and any other collaborators on your design, and are not visible to anyone else who views your design.

You can show notes when you present your design by clicking on presenter view. You can also download presentations and documents with notes attached.

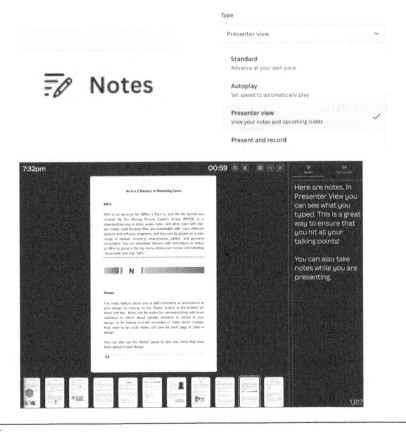

Notifications

Canva notifications are alerts that are sent to you by Canva to inform you of activity or updates related to your account or designs. Canva notifications can be delivered through a number of channels, including email, mobile push notifications, and in-app notifications.

Some examples of Canva notifications include:
- Team member activity notifications: If you are a member of a team in Canva, you may receive notifications when other team members make changes to designs or elements that you have access to.
- Comment notifications: If you have received a comment on one of your designs, you may receive a notification to let you know.
- Design updates: If you have made changes to a design and saved them, you may receive a notification to let you know that the design has been updated.
- Account updates: If there are updates to your Canva account or subscription, you may receive a notification to let you know.

You can manage your Canva notifications by going to your account settings and selecting the "Notifications" tab. From there, you can choose which notifications you want to receive, and how you want to receive them.

O

Opacity

A feature in Canva that allows you to adjust the transparency of an element, such as an image or graphic. It can be found in the top right of the toolbar and looks like a checkerboard.

Open in Desktop App

The "Open in Desktop App" feature in Canva allows you to open a design that you have created or edited in the web-based version of Canva in the Canva desktop app. The Canva desktop app is a separate application that you can download and install on your computer, and it provides additional features and functionality for designing and editing graphics.

To use the "Open in Desktop App" feature, you must first have the Canva desktop app installed on your computer. Then, while viewing a design in the web-based version of Canva, you can click on the "Open in Desktop App" button in the top right corner of the editor. This will open the design in the Canva desktop app, where you can continue working on it.

The "Open in Desktop App" feature is useful if you want to take advantage of the additional features and functionality of the desktop app, or if you prefer to work on your designs offline. It is also a good way to transfer designs between the web-based and desktop versions of Canva.

Order

The position of an element within a stack or layer. Canva allows you to adjust the order of elements in your designs. See also arrangement, send forward, send backward, and position.

Orientation

The direction in which an element is arranged, such as horizontally or vertically. Canva allows you to adjust the orientation of elements in your designs.

Outline

A design element in Canva that consists of a line around the edges of an element, such as text or a shape. In most instances you can change the width, and color of the outline.

Overlap

A technique in Canva that allows you to place one element on top of another, creating a layered effect.

P

Page Animations

Page animations in Canva are effects that can be added to the pages of a presentation or document to make them more dynamic and engaging. Page animations can include transitions between pages, such as fading in or out, or more complex effects such as slides or zooms.

To add page animations to a design in Canva, click on the "Animations" button in the toolbar at the top of the screen. This will open the animations panel on the right side of the screen, where you can choose from a variety of animation options. You can add an animation to a page by clicking on the "Add animation" button and selecting an animation from the list. You can then customize the animation settings, such as the duration and delay, to suit your needs.

Paint Effects

Paint Effect is an image filter that you can find by clicking on an element or photo you want to edit and then clicking "edit" in the top left toolbar. Scroll down until you find "paint effects" and apply it to your design.

Paint effect has several options and gives your elements and images the look of a painting when applied.

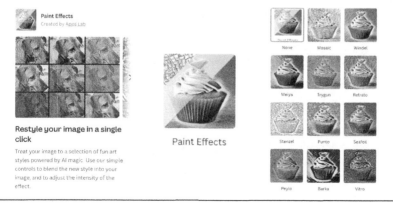

Palette

A feature in Canva that allows you to create a custom color palette for your design.

■■■

Pan

An animation option in Canva that allows you to move an image or graphic within the frame of your design.

■■■

Paste

"Paste" is a feature in Canva that allows you to paste text or objects from the clipboard into a design. This feature is useful for quickly adding content to a design or for copying content from one design to another.

1. Open the design that you want to add content to in the Canva editor.
2. Select the "Text" tool or the "Elements" you want to copy and paste.
3. Press the "Ctrl" and "X" keys on your keyboard to copy the content in the design.
4. Click on the location in the design where you want to paste the content.
5. Press the "Ctrl" and "V" keys on your keyboard to paste the content from the clipboard into the design.

Pattern

A pattern is a repeating set of shapes, lines, colors, or designs. Patterns can be found in nature, in art, in science, and in everyday life. Patterns can be used in many different ways, from creating beautiful artwork to helping us solve complex problems.

PDF

PDF stands for Portable Document Format.

PDF Editor

Canva's easy-to-use online PDF editor lets you quickly import, edit and convert your PDFs with no hassle. Our powerful editing features are designed to break up the PDF into individual elements that can be edited just like any other design asset. And when you're finished, you can share your work as a link, compress it into JPG, PNG or PDF files, or download it in a print-ready format. It's all available from the same dashboard.

Easy-to-use PDF editing tools

Edit PDF content fast
Take control of your edits by easily correcting typos; changing, adding or deleting text and images; or drawing lines, shapes, and signatures, without needing to switch between different tools.

Merge PDF files and organize pages with ease
Refresh the flow of your document with drag-and-drop tools to add, delete, rotate, and reorder pages.

Split, insert, extract PDF pages
Freshen up your page order with tools to blend content and change up your document structure.

Learn more here:
https://www.canva.com/pdf-editor/

PDF Print

In Canva, PDF Print downloads at a 300 dpi size, which is better quality for printing your documents. You can also add crop marks and bleeds to your design for professional printing.

PDF Standard

PDF is a standard for encoding documents in an "as printed" form that is portable between systems. It has a smaller file size but a lower resolution. It is great for sharing digitally.

Pen

A tool in Canva that allows you to draw freehand lines or shapes on your design. You can find the pen tool available in the draw app.

Pencil

A tool in Canva that allows you to draw freehand lines or shapes on your design with a pencil-like effect. You can find the pencil tool available in the draw app.

People

In the "People" section of Canva you can invite or remove people from your class, or team and update their roles.

.

To Add People:
- On the top corner of the homepage, click the gear icon to go to your Account Settings.
- From the side menu, click People.
- On the top corner of the page, click Invite people.
- Enter their email addresses.
- Click Send invitations.

Removing People or Changing their Roles:
- On the top corner of the homepage, click the gear icon to go to your Account Settings.
- From the side menu, click People.
- Click the role dropdown next to a person.
- To remove them from the team, select Remove from team.

To update their role, select a new role to change their access. Learn more about the different team roles and permissions.

Phone Wallpaper

Canva has templates so you customize your the background of your phone. You can select from one of the pre-designed templates that are available

Check out the templates here: https://www.canva.com/phone-wallpapers/templates/

Photo Editing

Canva has photo editing and photo enhancement tools that allow you to filter, add stickers, text, and auto touch-ups at the touch of a button. Each specific tool has been covered individually in this glossary. For more information go to individual photo filters, and features to learn more or click here: https://www.canva.com/photo-editor/

■■

Photogenic

Photogenic is a a photo filter available in Canva that offers several types of filters to get the desired tint or effect you are looking for. These include:

Natural	Soft
Warm	Vintage
Cool	Mono
Vivid	Color Pop

Natural

Mono

Fresco   Belvedere   Flint   Classic   Ink   Noir

Luna   Aero   Myst   Film   Newspaper   Slate

Picture Graph

A picture graph is a type of graph that uses symbols, such as pictures or icons, to represent data. Picture graphs are usually used to compare data across categories. For example, a picture graph might use images of cars to represent the number of cars sold per month in a particular market. Canva has the capabilities to create a picture graph in addition to 19 other graphs.

▪▪▪

Pie Chart

In Canva, you can create pie charts to represent data. A pie chart is a circular graph that divides a circle into proportional segments. Each segment represents a category of data and is usually colored. The size of the segment is proportional to the quantity or percentage of the data for that category. Pie charts are used to show the composition of a set of data, typically percentages of the whole. To create a pie chart go to elements and search "graphs" or "pie charts."

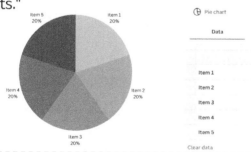

▪▪▪

Pixelate

Pixelate is a Canva photo editing feature that applies the lo-fi digital look of a pixelated image. To apply this style to an image, click on the image you want to pixelate, go to edit, and select "pixelate" from the options in your left vertical toolbar.

Planner

In Canva, there are close to 12,000 planner templates to help you stay organized. Whether it's a social media planner, a school planner, weekly planner, or more they have you covered.

Check out planner templates here:
https://www.canva.com/planners/templates/

PNG

A file format that stands for Portable Network Graphics. Canva allows you to save your designs as PNG files, which support transparent backgrounds and high-quality images.

Portrait

Portrait orientation is when the height of a page is greater than its width, like an 8.5 x 11 inch sheet of paper in a printer. It can also be used to describe an image or video that is taller than it is wide, such as a standard smartphone image.

In Canva you can filter elements in portrait orientation by going to the toggle bar in the right hand corner of the element search box and selecting on "vertical." You can also search "portrait."

 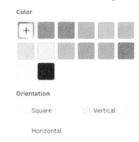

Position

In Canva, the term "position" refers to the location of an element within a design. You can adjust the position of elements in your design using Canva's alignment and spacing tools. For example, you can use these tools to align elements to the left, right, top, or bottom of the design, or to center them horizontally or vertically. You can also use the position tools to adjust the distance between elements, either by specifying an exact distance or by using predefined spacing options. Adjusting the position of elements in your design can help you create a balanced and visually appealing layout, and can also help you align elements with specific elements or areas of your design.

Poster

Canva's drag and drop poster maker makes it easy to design aesthetically pleasing posters with ease. They have over 100,000 poster pre-designed templates you can choose from or you can choose to make one from a blank canvas.

Create a poster from scratch here:
https://www.canva.com/create/posters/

· ·

Present

"Canva Present" is a feature in Canva that allows you to present a design as a slideshow. This feature is useful for showcasing designs, creating presentations, or giving demonstrations of designs that you have created in Canva.

To use the "Canva Present" feature in Canva:
1. Open the design that you want to present in the Canva editor.
2. Click on the "Share" button in the top right corner of the editor or use short cut keys. ⌥ ⌘ P
3. Select the "Present" option from the drop-down menu.
4. Use the arrow controls in the "Present" window to move through your presentation.
5. You can use the toolbar in the bottom to activate more features. .
6. To exit the presentation simply hit the "escape" button.

The "Canva Present" feature is a useful tool for showcasing designs, creating presentations, or giving demonstrations of designs that you have created in Canva. It can be particularly useful for designers who want to share their work with a wider audience or who want to create video content for social media or other platforms.

■■■

Present and Record

"Present and Record" is a feature in Canva that allows you to present a design as a slideshow and record the presentation for later viewing with a view link. You can also download the finished product as an MP4. This feature is useful for creating video presentations, tutorials, or demonstrations of designs that you have created in Canva.

To use the "Present and Record" feature in Canva:
1. Open the design that you want to present in the Canva editor.
2. Click on the "Share" button in the top right corner of the editor.
3. Select the "Present" button.
4. Select "Present and Record" from the drop menu and click "next."
5. Click on "Got to the Recording Studio" button to open up recording features.
6. You will need to select your camera and microphone options and then click on "Start Recording.'
7. When you stop recording be sure hit "save."
8. You can view your video or share the video with others using the link.

Important to note for Present and Record:

1. You can record on specific slides by selecting them from the thumbnails.
2. You can see your presenter notes in the studio which is helpful for writing out scripts for slides, or creating bulleted talking points.
3. You can pause and resume the video during the recording.
4. You can delete the video from the presentation and create a new one at a later date.

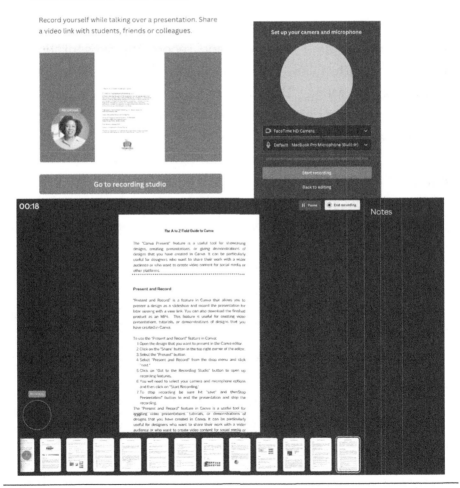

Presentation

A pre-designed template in Canva that you can use to create a professional-looking presentation. There are currently over 13,000 different styles to choose from, or you can create one from a blank canvas.

Read more information here:
https://www.canva.com/create/presentations/

Check out pre-designed templates here:
https://www.canva.com/templates/presentation

■■■

Presenter View

"Presenter View" is a feature in Canva that allows you to view a design as a presentation while also seeing speaker notes, a timer, the time, and other presentation tools. This feature is useful during presentations to remind you of slide notes, talking points, and to monitor the length of your presentation. It is recommended to have a second display when using this feature.

To use the "Presenter View" feature in Canva:
1. Open the design that you want to present in the Canva editor.
2. Click on the "Present" button in the top right corner of the editor.
3. Select the "Presenter View" from the drop down bar.
4. Click on the "X" button or "escape" button to end the presentation view.

The "Presenter View" feature in Canva is a useful tool for sharing presentations. This is a great option for using a dual display. You view your presenter notes, the time, a timer, and thumbnails of your slides to easily navigate your presentation. You can also launch Canva.Live, pause your presentation and access magic keys or a hot keys menu to add animations.

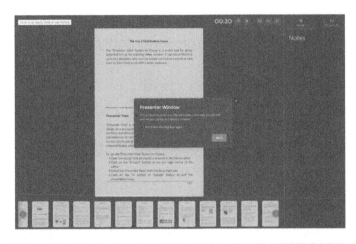

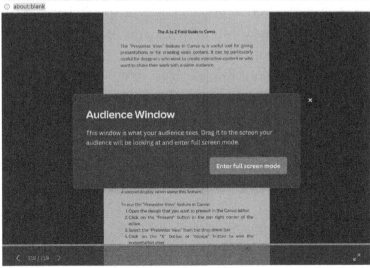

Preview

The "Preview" feature allows you to view your design as it will appear when it is published or exported. This can be useful for getting a sense of how your design will look in its final form, or for checking that everything is positioned and formatted correctly.

To use the "Preview" feature in Canva, click on the perpendicular "Preview" arrows in the bottom menu of the editor. This will open a new window showing a full-screen preview of your design. You can use the preview to view your design as it will appear on different devices and at different sizes, and to see how it looks when printed or exported.

The "Preview" feature is a good way to get a sense of how your design will look when it is finished, and to catch any issues or mistakes that you might have missed while working on the design. You can use it to make any final adjustments or changes before publishing or exporting your design.

Print

Canva Print is a service provided by Canva that allows you to print a wide range of physical products, including business cards, brochures, t-shirts, posters, and more.

To see everything Canva prints go to https://www.canva.com/print/.

To print a design you have created in Canva simply go to "share" and "print my design." Select the type of print product you want to create. You may have to resize and reformat your design to fit that type of product.

Canva Print offers a wide range of customization options and high-quality printing at competitive prices. You can use Canva Print to print marketing materials, promotional items, or any other products you need.

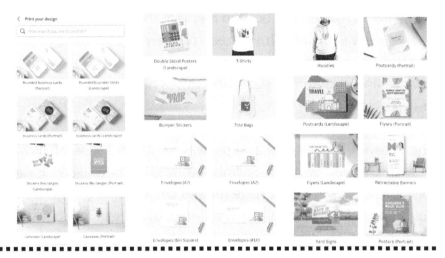

Print Bleed

In Canva, you can add bleed to a design by increasing the size of the canvas beyond the finished size of the product. When creating a design with bleed in Canva, it is important to make sure that any elements that extend to the edge of the page are extended beyond the finished size of the product by at least the amount of bleed specified by the printer. This will ensure that the design prints correctly and that there are no white borders around the edge of the finished product.

Prisma

Prisma is a Canva photo editing feature that a painting filter to your images using AI technology. To apply this style to an image, click on the image you want to add a paint filter to go to edit, and select "Prisma" from the options in your left vertical toolbar.

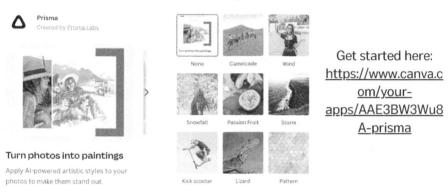

Get started here: https://www.canva.com/your-apps/AAE3BW3Wu8A-prisma

Turn photos into paintings

Apply AI-powered artistic styles to your photos to make them stand out.

Productivity

In the "Discover Apps" section of Canva the app catalogue can be further filtered by categories. Productivity is one of the category filters for apps that integrate into Canva. It is geared toward platforms and tools that you can import media from.

See Productivity Apps here: https://www.canva.com/your-apps/import-media

Progress Bar

A progress bar graph is a graphical representation of progress over time. Progress bar graphs are often used in project management and other fields to show the progress of tasks or projects over a period of time. You can find the progress bar in Canva by searching "progress bar" in elements.

Progress Dial

A progress dial chart, also known as a "gauge chart" or "speedometer chart", is a type of chart that is used to display the progress of a task or goal in the form of a dial or gauge. It typically consists of a dial or gauge, with a needle or marker that points to the current progress on a circular scale. The scale is usually divided into segments, with each segment representing a specific range of progress. Progress dial charts are often used in dashboards and other visualization tools to display progress in real-time. You can find a progress dial by searching "progress dial" in Canva elements.

Progress Ring

A progress ring chart, also known as a "ring chart" is a type of chart that is used to display the progress of a task or goal in the form of a ring or donut shape. It typically consists of a ring or donut shape, with a portion of the ring filled in to indicate the current progress. The progress is usually represented as a percentage, with the filled-in portion of the ring representing the percentage of the task that has been completed. Progress ring charts are often used in dashboards and other visualization tools to display progress in real-time, and can be an alternative to the traditional progress bar or dial chart. You can find the progress ring by searching in elements using "progress ring."

Projects

The Projects folder can be found in the "Home" section of your Canva dashboard. All of your projects, folders, designs, images, and brand templates can be found here by clicking on the folder. You can further filter your search for templates and assets by clicking on each subcategory.

Proposal

A proposal is a type of template in Canva that presents a plan or suggestion for a specific project, program, or course of action. It is typically used to persuade or convince a person or group of people to accept or support the proposed plan or idea. Proposals can be written for a variety of purposes, such as business, research, or funding, and are often used in the fields of sales, marketing, and project management. A proposal typically includes an introduction, background information, a description of the proposed plan or idea, a discussion of the potential benefits and drawbacks, and a conclusion. It may also include a budget, a timeline, and supporting materials such as charts, graphs, and references.

Check out these proposal templates:
https://www.canva.com/proposals/templates/

Prototype

In Canva, a prototype is a simulation of a user interface or product that allows you to test and preview how it will function and look. Prototyping can be a useful tool for designers and product teams to get a sense of how a product will work and to identify any issues or improvements that need to be made before the product is fully developed.

To create a prototype in Canva, you will need to use the prototyping tools in the Canva editor. These tools allow you to link together different pages or screens in your design to create a simulated user flow or experience including linkable elements, animations, buttons, and wireframes. You can also add interactions and animations to the prototype to make it more realistic.

Read more about prototyping here:
https://www.canva.com/prototypes/

Desktop prototypes
From online stores to sign-up pages and ads—build something for every device.

Mobile prototypes
Design apps and websites with ready made mobile UI prototyping kits.

Tablet prototypes
Sculpt responsive apps that impress on tablet devices.

Share

Brand template | Present | View-only link | Template link

Present and record | Copy to clipboard | QR Code | Save to folder

Send to phone | Embed | Website | Share link to watch

Prototype

Publish Assignment

In Canva for Education you can create and publish assignments for students to complete within Canva.

To do this:

- Create or open an existing design for the assignment.
- From the top corner of the editor, click Share.
- Scroll down until you find Assignment and Click on it.
- Under Choose where students should submit work, select Canva from the dropdown.
- Under Share as, select New design for each student.
- Add the assignment instructions. It will be attached to the assignment template, and students will see it. Click Next.
- Choose who the assignment is for. On the text field, type a class, group, or individual student names.
- Click Publish to finish.
-

You can create a new design for each student to work on individually, or you can send the design as instructions only. Instructions only versions will only allow students to view the materials. They will not be able to edit the design.

The A to Z Field Guide to Canva

Screenshots of how to post an assignment:

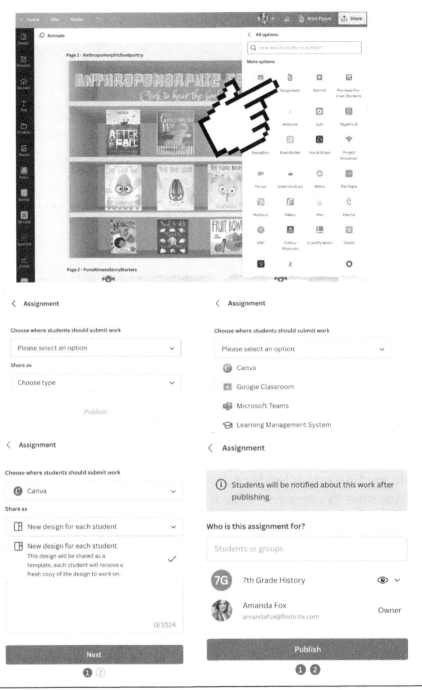

Purchase

If you are using a free version of Canva there are premium elements and features that have to be purchased for use. When you use these premium elements in your designs, they'll be watermarked until you buy them. You will be prompted to purchase these assets prior to downloading your design. You can always upgrade up to avoid individual element costs.

Purchase History

In Canva you can access all of your previous purchases and their respective invoices issued by going to Account Settings. This includes any premium elements and print order purchases. You also receive a copy of your invoice in your email every time you're charged.

You can also filter your purchase history by type so it only shows your print orders.

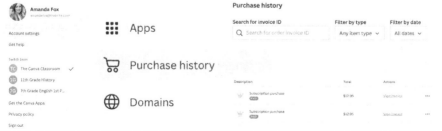

Q

QR Code

In the apps section of Canva you can search for QR Code generator and turn any link into a QR code by adding the link to the box and clicking "generate."

Quick Create

Canva Quick Create is a feature in Canva that allows you to quickly create new designs using pre-designed templates for social media. You can create up to 8 designs at once. With Canva Quick Create, you can choose from a variety of templates and design elements to create professional-looking designs in just a few clicks, and team users can add a logo and use the brand kit when designing.

To use Canva Quick Create:
1. Go to the Canva homepage and click on the "Social Media" option.
2. Click on "Quick Create Collection."
3. Click "Get started"
4. Select up to 8 different formats you want to use and click

continue.

5. Customize the text, Image and Logo, template, and style and hit "finished."

6. See your designs in your home dashboard or under "projects."

Canva Quick Create is a fast and easy way to create professional-looking designs in Canva, and is particularly useful for users who are new to design or who need to create designs quickly. It offers a wide range of templates and design elements to choose from, making it easy to create a wide variety of designs in a short amount of time.

Learn more here:
https://www.canva.com/help/quick-create-social-media/

R

Radial Progress

A radial progress bar chart is an interactive visualization that displays progress or completion of a task in a circular format. It features an arc that is filled in as the task progresses and can also be used to indicate how far a user has progressed within an application, how much of a task has been completed, or how close a user is to achieving a goal. You can find radial progress bars in the elements search and use the key word "radial progress" or "chart".

Recent Designs

In the "Home" dashboard in Canva you can find all your recent designs at the top of the platform. Anything you recently created will show up under "recent designs." This is a great way to search newly created designs quickly.

Recently Used

In the elements tab in the left vertical toolbar, you can find all photos, videos, and graphics you have recently used in previous designs.

Recolor

A term in Canva when you change the color of an element, such as an image or graphic.

Redo

The "Redo" feature allows you to reverse the effects of the "Undo" command and reapply an action that you have undone. This can be useful if you have made a change to your design and then undone it by mistake, or if you want to revert to a previous version of your design after making multiple changes.

To use the "Redo" feature in Canva, click on the "Redo" button in the top menu of the editor. This will reapply the most recent action that you undone using the "Undo" button. You can also use the keyboard shortcut "Ctrl+Y" (on Windows) or "Command+Y" (on Mac) to redo an action.

Keep in mind that the "Redo" feature only works for actions that have been undone using the "Undo" button or keyboard shortcut. If you have saved your design or closed the editor since making a change, you will not be able to redo that action.

Remote Control

The remote control feature allows multiple presenters to control slides in real-time with Remote Control. To use the remote control, simply go into one of the present modes and find the "share remote control" option in the bottom right hand corner of your screen. Next copy the link to present from another device. Anyone with the link can switch slides and navigate the presentation.

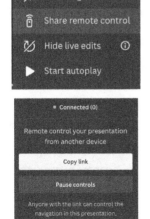

Pro-tip: I typically share the link in my notes tab or message it to co-presenters. The link will work if you exit out of the presentation to share the link and re-enter present mode. .

Review Student Work

Canva for Education allows students to submit work directly to you for review. You'll be notified via email when students complete assignments that you published on Canva.

Here's how to review them:
1. From the notification email, click Review. On Canva, you can find assignments that need reviewing on your Classwork folder.
2. Review the assignment. You can leave comments directly on their work (optional).
3. Once done, from the top corner of the editor, click Review.
4. This is optional, but may be relevant for Step 5: Type a message or feedback for the student.
5. If you want the student to make further changes in their homework, click Give feedback. If you're happy with their work, click Return. (examples below have student's names blacked out.

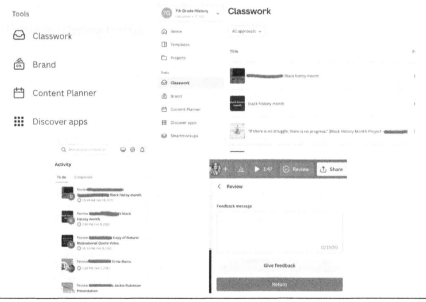

Remove Background

A tool in Canva that allows you to remove the background from an image or graphic, leaving just the subject of the image. You can also uses the restore and erase tool if needed to add parts that were removed.

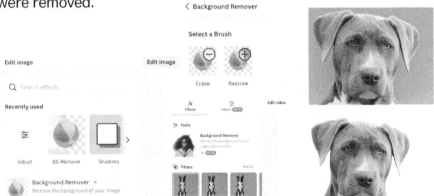

Resize

In Canva, the "Resize" feature allows you to change the dimensions of your design or the individual elements within your design. This can be useful if you need to resize your design to fit a specific size or aspect ratio, or if you want to change the size of an element to better fit within your layout.

To resize and element, click and drag any crop handle to adjust what part of the element you want to be visible. You can also resize the element within the crop space.

Resize and Copy

In Canva, the "Resize and Copy" feature allows you to create multiple copies of a design that are different sizes. This can be useful if you want to create a series of differently-sized files that are all based on the same design, such as a set of social media posts with different dimensions (also see Quick Create for social media posts).

You simply put the new custom size or dimensions in the width and height and either create a copy with new dimensions or resize your current design.

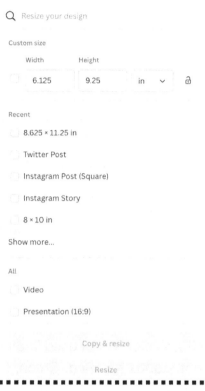

Restore Image

When you have edited an image in Canva you can restore the image to its original state by clicking on "restore image" in the top dashboard.

Resume

In Canva, a resume template is a pre-formatted document that can be used as a starting point for creating a resume. It usually includes sections for contact information, work experience, education, and other relevant information. There are over 11,000 pre-designed templates that allow users to customize the appearance, text, and overall layout of the resume to make it more visually appealing and tailored to their needs.

Check out Resume Templates:
 https://www.canva.com/resumes/templates/

■■■

RGB

RGB is color model used in digital graphics and on-screen purposes that stands for "Red, Green, Blue." Canva allows you to adjust the RGB values of an element to create a specific color. You change between RGB and CMYK when downloading a design. RGB is best for designs intended for digital sharing, while CMYK color values are best for printed designs.

■■■

Rulers

In Canva, rulers can be added to a design to help with alignment and sizing of elements. To turn on ruler view to to "File" and then click on "view settings." Select "Show Rulers and Margins."

S

Saturation

Saturation in Canva design is a common term that refers to the intensity or vividness of color in an image. It is the purity of a color and is determined by the number of gray tones in an image. Increasing the saturation in an image will make the colors appear stronger, more intense, and more vibrant. Conversely, decreasing saturation will make the colors appear softer, subtler, and less vibrant.

Save

A feature in Canva that allows you to save your design progress and continue working on it later. Canva autosaves your designs, but it is also a good idea to hit save before exiting.

Save to Folder

"Save to folder" is a feature that allows you to save a design to a specific folder within your Canva account. When you save a design to a folder, it will be added to that folder and organized with any other designs that you have saved to that folder.

To save a design to a folder in Canva, click on the "File" menu and select "Save to folder." This will open a window where you can select the folder that you want to save the design to, or you can create a new folder. Once you have selected a folder, click "Save" to add the design to that folder.

Folders in Canva can be a useful way to organize your designs and keep them separate from one another. You can create different folders for different projects, clients, or categories of designs, and then save your designs to the appropriate folders. This can make it easier to find and access your designs later on.

Read more here: https://www.canva.com/help /manage-folder-contents/

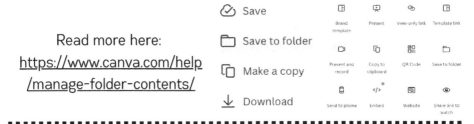

Schedule

The schedule feature in Canva allows you to schedule posts to be published on social media at a later date and time. This can be useful if you want to plan your social media content in advance and have it automatically published at a specific time, rather than having to remember to manually post it yourself. To use the schedule feature in Canva, you will need to connect your social media accounts to your Canva account and then choose the date and time that you want your post to be published.

Find out more about scheduling posts here: https://www.canva.com/help/content-planner/

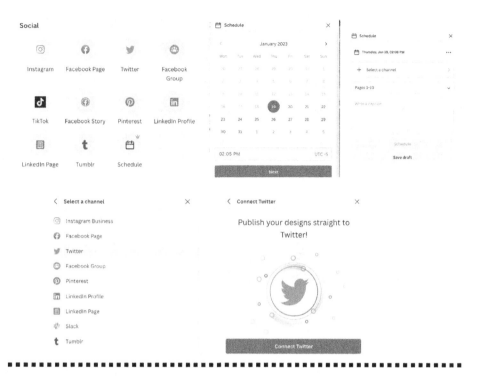

Screen Recorder

In addition to being able to record yourself and present, you can also exit your presentation and record and share your screen on the camera. You can edit and trim your videos in your design with Canva's free online video recorder to ensure you have perfectly timed content and tutorials.

To record your screen click the "Uploads" tab on the menu and press Record Yourself on your browser. On your laptop, you can choose between Camera Only and Screen Share to include a screen recording.

Find out more about screen recording here:
https://www.canva.com/features/online-video-recorder/

Select

A feature in Canva that allows you to choose one or more elements in your design to edit or manipulate. Simply use your track pad or mouse to drag a capture window over the elements you want to select. From there you can resize, recolor, change fonts, or group items together.

Send Backward

"Send Backward" is a feature in Canva that allows you to move an object or design element backward in the stacking order. This feature is useful for adjusting the layering of objects or design elements in a design.

To use the "Send Backward" feature in Canva:

1. Open the design that you want to edit in the Canva editor.
2. Select the object or design element that you want to move backward.
3. Click on the "Position" button in the toolbar on the right.
4. Select the "Send Backward" option from the drop-down menu.
5. The selected object or design element will be moved backward in the stacking order.

The "Send Backward" feature in Canva is a useful tool for adjusting the layering of objects or design elements in a design.

See also "Position."

Send to Back

The "Send to Back" feature allows you to move an object or layer behind all other objects or layers on the canvas.

To use this feature:

1. Select the object or layer that you want to move to the back.
2. Click on the "Position" button in the top menu.
3. From the dropdown menu, select "Send to Back".
4. The selected object or layer will now be moved behind all other objects or layers on the canvas.

You can also use the "Send Backward" option to move an object or layer one step back, or the "Bring Forward" option to move an object or layer one step forward.

Send to Phone

"Send to phone" in Canva is a feature that allows you to send a design that you have created in Canva to your phone as an image. This can be useful if you want to quickly view or share your design on your phone, or if you want to use it as a reference while you are away from your computer.

To use the "Send to phone" feature in Canva, you will need to go to the "Share" tab in the top right corner of the editor and click on the "Send to phone" button. This will open a window where you can scan a QR code to open the design on your phone. You can also have the design sent as an email.

The "Send to phone" feature can be a useful tool for quickly and easily accessing your designs on your phone. It can also be useful for sharing designs with others or using them as a reference while you are on the go.

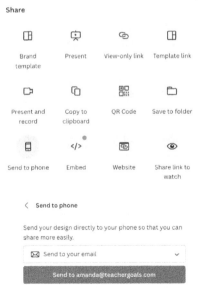

Shadows

"Shadows" are a design effect in Canva that adds a shadow to an element, such as an image or graphic, giving it a sense of depth or dimensionality.

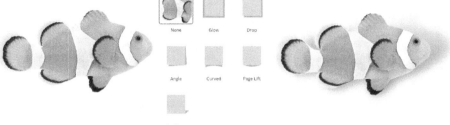

Shape

A design element in Canva that consists of a closed path with straight or curved lines, such as a rectangle, circle, or star. You can find shapes in the element toolbar in the left vertical column and search "shape."

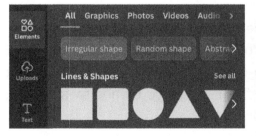

Share

A button in Canva that allows you to share your designs with others, either by sending a link or by exporting the design to a file. There are many ways to share your designs.

Share on Social

"Canva Share on social" is a feature in Canva that allows you to share designs that you have created in Canva directly to social media platforms. This feature can be accessed from the "Share" menu in the top right corner of the Canva editor.

To share a design on social media using Canva click on the "Share" button in the top right corner of the editor and select the "Share on social" option from the drop-down menu. You can connect and choose the social media platform where you want to share the design from the options available.

Also, see schedule posts. Read more about social media sharing limitations here:
https://www.canva.com/help/sharing-social-media-limitations/

Share With Me

In your Canva "Home" dashboard click on "Projects" and choose "shared with me" from the dropdown box to access all the designs that have been shared with you.

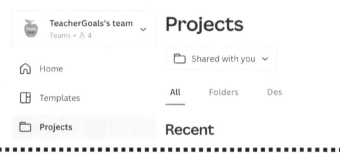

Single Sign On and Security

Canva Teams and Canva for Education administrators can set up "single sign on" for their organization. This enables Canva users to automatically have their email domain recognized and will add them to the Team or School/District.

This can expedite teacher verification for Canva for Education accounts.

If you are an admin learn more here: https://www.canva.com/help/set-up-sso/

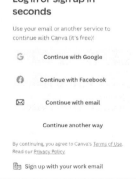

Slideshow Video

Canva has a slideshow maker that you can use to create engaging videos. You can use your own photos, or choose from their free stock library, add text, and animations.

You can download the slideshows as Gifs, videos, share links, or share them live using presenter view. You can even have them autoplay.

Read more here:
https://www.canva.com/create/slideshows/

•••

Smartmockups

Canva Smartmockups are pre-designed mockup templates that allow you to quickly and easily create professional-looking product mockups in Canva. With Canva Smartmockups, you can choose from a wide range of templates featuring different product types, such as t-shirts, business cards, and phone cases, and customize them with your own design.

To use Canva Smartmockups:
1. Go to the Canva homepage and click on the "Smartmockups" tab or select "smartmockups" from "Share" options in a preexisting design.
2. Select the type of product mockup that you want to create, such as a t-shirt or business card.
3. Choose a template from the available options, or start with a blank canvas.

4. Upload your design to the template using the "Uploads" tab in the toolbar on the left.

5. Customize the template using the design tools and elements in Canva.

6. Click the "Create" button to save your mockup.

Canva Smartmockups are a fast and easy way to create professional-looking product mockups in Canva, and are particularly useful for designers, marketers, and businesses who need to showcase their products in a professional way. They offer a wide range of templates and design elements to choose from, making it easy to create a wide variety of mockups in a short amount of time.

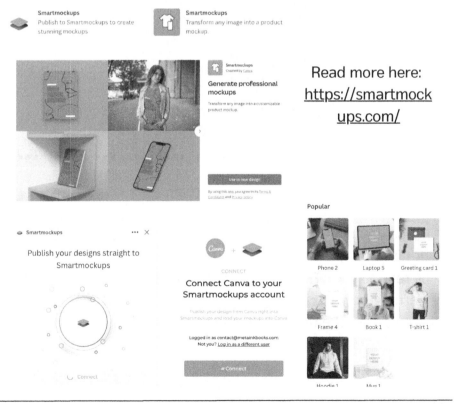

Read more here:
https://smartmock ups.com/

Smooth

While Canva doesn't currently have a "smooth" feature you can achieve a smooth edged effect in images by applying the blur feature. See "blur."

Snap

When a photo or image automatically fills a frame or grid it is said to "snap" inside of it. You can detach the image from the frame by double clicking on the photo and selecting "detach image."

Speech

When you are in a Canva design you can double click on any text in the design and a toolbar will pop up. Select "speech" and the text will be read to you. This is great for differentiation or for users that are learning how to read or speak another language. Additionally, you can convert the text to other languages.

Starred

You can star any items found in elements such as graphics, videos, or images and they will be curated in your "starred" folder. To star an element you simply click on the three dots in the top right hand corner of the element and select "star" from the drop down selection. You can find all "starred" elements in your "starred" folders

Sticker

In Canva, the term sticker refers to multiple things. Canva has a sticker maker that helps you create stickers that can be printed by Canva print.

It also refers to cutout graphics that can be searched in Canva elements. These stickers can be added to any design.

Learn more about designing and printing your own stickers here: https://www.canva.com/stickers/

Sticky Notes

In Canva, you can create and add custom sticky notes to brainstorm designs or whiteboards so teammates and peer and visualize your ideas. You can find sticky notes in the elements tab by searching "sticky notes" to create designs built for collaboration.

Learn more about sticky notes here:

https://www.canva.com/features/sticky-notes/

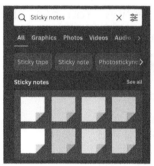

Stock Photos

Stock photos in Canva are professional images that you can download and use in your designs. They include a wide range of subjects, from people, places, and objects, to abstract images and more. With Canva's library of over 1 million stock photos and illustrations, it's easy to find the perfect photo to express yourself in your design. You can find them under elements and filtering "photos" or by going to their gallery of photos that gives you more filtering options: https://www.canva.com/photos/free/

Styles

Styles refer to pre-designed visual elements that can be applied to text, shapes, and other design elements to quickly create a cohesive and professional-looking design. Styles can include things like preset color schemes, font combinations, and graphic elements such as textured backgrounds and borders.

Canva has a wide variety of styles available, ranging from simple and minimalistic to bold and eye-catching. You can access the styles by clicking on the "Design" tab in the side panel on the left side of the Canva editor and switching to "Styles." From there, you can browse through the available styles and apply them to your design elements by clicking on the style that you want to use. You can also find the color palette of any brand kits that you have created.

Using styles can save you time and effort when designing, as you don't have to create all of the visual elements from scratch. They can also help to ensure that your design has a cohesive and professional look, as all of the elements are designed to work together.

SVG

An SVG (short for "scalable vector graphic") is a type of image file that is used to display graphics and visual content on the web. Unlike raster image formats (such as JPG or PNG), which are made up of pixels and have fixed dimensions, SVG images are vector-based and can be scaled to any size without losing quality. This makes SVG images ideal for use on the web, where they can be resized to fit different screen sizes and devices without losing quality. You can download designs as an SVG in Canva by clicking on "download" in the top dashboard above your canvas and selecting "SVG."

Switch Teams

"Switch Teams" is a feature in Canva that allows you to switch between different teams or organizations that you are a member of within Canva. This feature is useful for designers who are a member of multiple teams or organizations and who need to access the designs and resources of each team or organization.

To use the "Switch Teams" feature in Canva:

1. Click on the "Teams" button in the top left corner of the Canva editor.
2. Select the team or organization that you want to switch to from the list of teams.
3. The Canva editor will switch to the selected team or organization.

148

T

Tables

Tables in Canva are a way to organize and present data in a grid format. They can be used to create a variety of documents such as spreadsheets, charts, and infographics. Canva tables are designed to be highly customizable, and users can easily add or remove rows and columns, change the colors and font styles, and add images or graphics. Users can also import data from Excel or Google Sheets to create tables in Canva. The tables can be used to create tables in documents, presentations, flyers, brochures, social media posts and many other design elements.

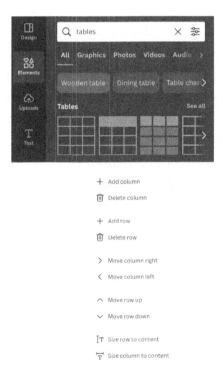

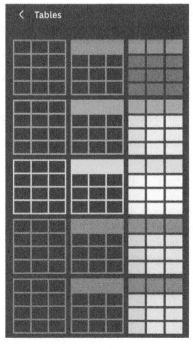

Teacher Verification

Teacher verification with Canva is a process that allows educators to verify their teaching status and access certain resources and features that are only available to verified teachers. To verify their teaching status, educators must provide proof that they are currently employed as a teacher at an accredited educational institution.

The purpose of teacher verification with Canva is to ensure that the resources and features that are available to teachers are being used for educational purposes, and to provide a way for educators to access resources and support that are tailored to their needs.

To verify their teaching status with Canva, educators can visit the Canva website and click on the "Education" link in the top menu. From there, they can follow the prompts to apply for teacher verification and provide the required documentation. Once their teaching status has been verified, educators will have access to additional resources and features such as custom templates, lesson plans, and professional development opportunities.

Learn more about Canva for Education and getting verified here:
https://www.canva.com/help/about-canva-for-education/Official

Official teacher identification that shows current status, like the following:

- Photo or scan of a license/certification indicating teaching qualification
- Photo or scan showing employment status at a school (e.g. letter of employment)
- Photo or scan of school ID indicating teaching status
- Photo or scan of Google Certified Educator or Google Certified Trainer certification
- Document proving an organization's status as a government recognized, formally accredited K-12 (primary, secondary, or pre-college) educational institution

Team Templates

Brand template   Present   Template link   View-only link

In Canva for Teams or Canva for Education you have access to thousands of professionally designed templates. You can also create your own branded templates for the whole team to use, or import existing templates into Canva. Multiple team members can work on the same design and allowing anyone to provide feedback, tag, share, and resolve edits anytime, anywhere, on any device. To share your template with a team you can easily add it to a team folder or hit "share" and select "branded template."

To find a team or branded template go to your "Home" dashboard, and select "Brand." Under the brand tab select "branded templates."

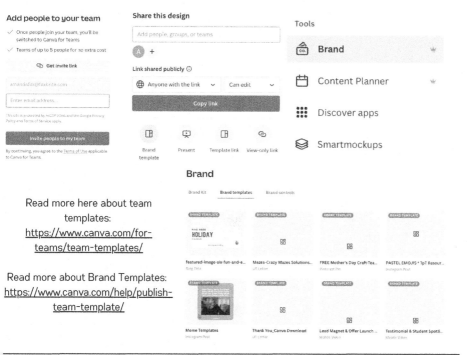

Read more here about team templates:
https://www.canva.com/for-teams/team-templates/

Read more about Brand Templates:
https://www.canva.com/help/publish-team-template/

Templates

In Canva, a template is a pre-designed layout that you can use as a starting point for creating a new design. Templates can include text, graphics, and other design elements, and can be customized to fit your specific needs. You can choose from a wide range of templates in Canva, including templates for social media posts, presentations, business documents, and more. Templates can help you save time by providing a professional-looking foundation for your designs, and can also help you ensure that your designs are consistent and follow best practices for layout and design.

Templates can filtered and searched in the Canva dashboard by keyword or type of template you are looking for. In the left hand tool bar there are dropdown options to refine your search.

⌂   Home

⊞   All templates

>   **Business**

>   Social Media

>   Video

>   Marketing

>   Custom Prints

>   Cards & Invitations

>   Education

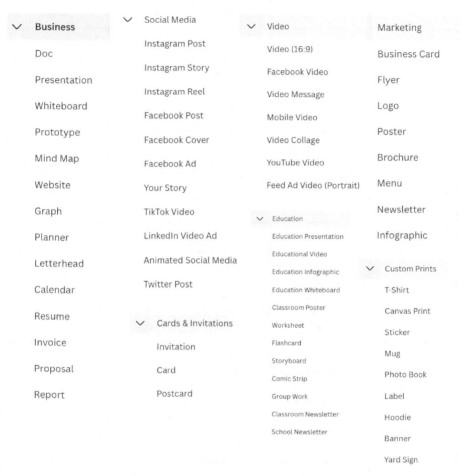

From here each type of template then provides you with pre-designed examples that you can start from.

You can also use keyword search to find themed templates.

The next few pages include tables with keywords to search for pre-designed templates in Canva. You can find the interactive hyperlinked pages at the link below:

https://www.canva.com/html_sitemap/

The A to Z Field Guide to Canva

3d	Bbq	Bunny	Circle Frame	Covid
Abstract	Beach	Business	Circle Sticker	Cow
Aesthetic	Beauty	Butterfly	City	Cricket
Aesthetic Background	Bee	Cafe	Class	Cross
Animal	Before And After	Cake	Cleaning	Crown
Anime	Bible	Camping	Closed	Culture
Anniversary	Bike	Candy	Clothes	Cupcake
Apple	Biology	Car	Cloud	Cute
April	Bird	Carnival	Clouds	Dance
April Fools	Birthday	Carousel	Coffee	Dark
Art	Black	Cartoon	College	Date
Article	Black Friday	Cat	Colorful	
Ash Wednesday	Black History Month	Celebration	Coming Soon	Dental
Autumn	Blog	Chemistry	Communication	Diamond
Award	Blue	Children	Company	Did You Know
Baby Shower	Blur	Chinese	Computer	Diet
Bakery	Boho	Chocolate	Confetti	Dinosaur
Balloons	Brain	Christmas	Congratulations	Disco
Bank	Brown	Christmas Wishlist	Construction	Dj
Bar	Brush	Church	Contact Us	Doctor
Baseball	Budget	Cinco De Mayo	Cooking	Dog
Basketball	Building	Circle	Countdown	Dogs

The A to Z Field Guide to Canva

Dots	Fireworks	Goals	Heart	Jewelry
Easter	Fish	God	Help	Job
Easter Bunny	Fitness	Gold	Hiring	Kids
Easter Egg	Flower	Golf	History	Labor Day
Eid	Food	Good Friday	Holiday Wishlist	Laptop
Eid Mubarak	Food Logo	Good Morning	Holy Week	Law
Elegant	Football	Gradient	Home	Leaf
English	Forest	Gradients	Honey	Lent
Environment	Fourth Of July	Graduation	Horror	Library
Event	Frames	Graphic Design	Horse	Life
Eyes	Friday	Graphs	Hospital	Lips
Facial	Friends	Green	Hotel	Log
Fall	Fruit	Grid	House	Lohri
Family	Fun	Gym	Human	Love
Farm	Galaxy	Hair	Ice Cream	Makeup
Fashion	Game	Halloween	Independence Day	Man
Fathers Day	Gaming	Hand	Independence Day India	Mandala
Feedback	Garden	Happy Holi	International Womens Day	Map
Festival	Geometric	Happy Holidays	Introduction	March
Film	Giveaway	Happy Lohri	Isra Miraj	Mardi Gras
Finance	Glitter	Header	It	Marketing
Fire	Globe	Health	January	Marriage

The A to Z Field Guide to Canva

Masjid	Navratri	People	Price List	Robot
Math	Neon	Perfume	Process	Running
Mathematics	News	Pet	Product	Safety
Medical	Newspaper	Phone	Prom	Sale
Medicine	New Year	Photo	Promo	Sales
Meeting	Notes	Photography	Promotion	Sand
Memorial Day	November	Physics	Property	Scary
Mental Health	Numbers	Pin	Pumpkin	School
Message	Nutrition	Pink	Purple	Science
Mind	Ocean	Pink Background	Puzzle	Selamat Hari Raya
Minimalist	October	Pizza	Quote	Self Care
Mockup	Office	Plan	Rainbow	September
Modern	Open House	Plane	Ramadan	Shop
Mom	Orange	Planet	Ramadan Mubarak	Shopping
Mood	Painting	Plants	Real Estate	Simple
Moon	Palm Sunday	Podcast	Red	Skin Care
Mosque	Party	Poem	Reminder	Smoke
Mothers Day	Passover	Polaroid	Research	Snow
Motivation	Pastel	Pongal	Restaurant	Soccer
Mountain	Pattern	Pool	Retro	Spa
Music	Pen	Portrait	Review	Space
Nature	Pencil	Prayer	Road	Spooky

The A to Z Field Guide to Canva

Sports	Tea	Vintage	World Sleep Day
Spotify	Teacher	Vision Board	Yellow
Spring	Team	Volleyball	Yoga
Stamp	Tech	Volunteer	
Star	Technology	Wall	
Store	Testimonial	Water	
Strawberry	Tiger	Watercolor	
Student	Time	Wave	
Study	Timetable	Waves	
Subscribe	Title	Webinar	
Success	To Do List	Wedding	
Summer	Travel	Welcome	
Sun	Tree	White	
Sunflower	Trees	Win	
Sunglasses	Triangle	Wine	
Sunrise	Trip	Winter	
Superbowl	Ugadi	Women	
Superhero	Ukraine	Womens Day	
Survey	Unicorn	Workshop	
Sushi	University	World	
Table	Veterans Day	World Health Day	
Tarot	Video Background	World Peace Day	

Template Link

A template link in Canva is a URL that allows someone to access a Canva design and use it as a starting point for a new design. This can be useful if you want to share a design that you have created with others, and allow them to use it as a template for their own projects.

When someone clicks on a template link, they will be able to access the design in their web browser and make a copy of it. They will then be able to edit the copy and use it as a starting point for their own design.

Template links can be a useful way to share your designs with others and allow them to use them as a starting point for their own projects. They can save time and effort by providing a pre-designed template that can be customized for a specific purpose. This is a great option for sharing assignments with students.

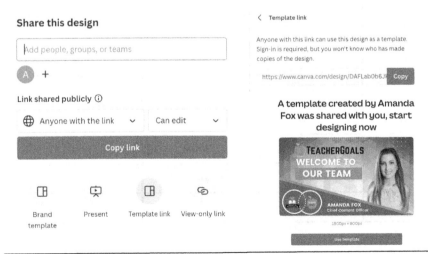

Text Box

Text box in Canva is a feature that allows users to add text boxes to their designs. The text boxes can be used to add titles, descriptions, quotes, or any other type of text to a design. Text box in Canva also allows users to customize the text box size, font, color, alignment, and other design elements.

Text Effects

In Canva, "text effects" are visual effects that you can apply to text to alter its appearance. Text effects can be used to add emphasis, create visual interest, or change the overall look and feel of your text.

To apply a text effect in Canva:
1. Select the text box that you want to apply a text effect to.
2. Click on the "Text" button in the top menu.
3. From the dropdown menu, select "Effects".
4. A submenu will appear, allowing you to choose from a variety of text effects.
5. Select the text effect that you want to apply, and it will be applied to the selected text box. You can adjust the settings for the text effect using the options that appear on the right side of the screen.

Canva offers a wide range of text effects to choose from, including basic effects like "Bold" and "Italic", as well as more creative effects like "Shadow" and "Outline". You can experiment with different text effects to find the one that best suits your needs. Once you click on a text effect there are more options to future customize the look.

Please note that text effects are applied to the entire text box, and cannot be applied to specific words or characters within the text. If you want to apply a text effect to only part of your text, you will need to create a separate text box for that portion of the text.

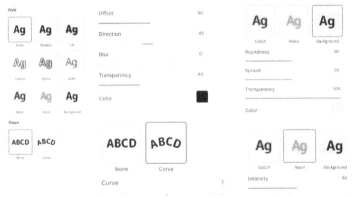

Text to Image

Text to Image is an AI app that integrations with Canva and allows you to type a prompt and the text is converted magically into an image.

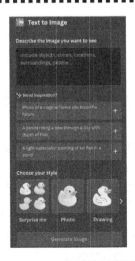

Thumbnail

Thumbnail in Canva is an image used to represent a larger design. It is usually a smaller version of the original image that is used as a preview and helps viewers to quickly identify what the design is about. Thumbnails are usually displayed in a grid or list format, and can be used to link to the full-sized image.

There are over 13,000 templates for thumbnails for Youtube videos.

Check them out here:
https://www.canva.com/templates/?query=thumbnail

■■

Thumbnail View

Thumbnail view allows you enter in a scrolling view of all of your pages in a design below the design canvas. You can use shortcuts to enter thumbnail view to easily navigate between pages and slides.

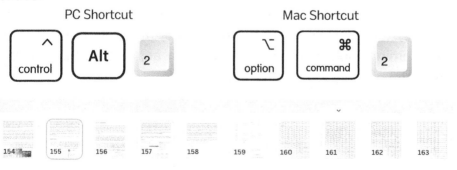

Tidy Up

Space evenly

□ Vertically |□| Horizontally

||| Tidy up   ⌥⇧T

In Canva, "tidy up" is the act of organizing and arranging elements in your design to create an orderly, professional-looking composition. To achieve this, Canva offers several tools and features, like alignment and spacing, which allow you to align elements to specific points and adjust the space between them.

You can also use the grouping and layering tools to organize elements into logical groups or layers, making it easier to work with and edit your design. By tidying up your designs in Canva, you can create cohesive, well-organized layouts that are easy to read and understand.

 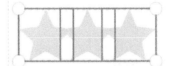

Timed Animations (Show Time)

Timing your animations is possible in video templates. When you page, text, or element animations you can view timeline by double clicking your keyboard or right clicking your mouse to bring up the "show timing" option. From here you can adjust the duration by sliding the element to suit your timed needs.

○ Animate

◔ Show timing

↻ Comment   ⌥⌘N

Transparency

Transparency can be adjusted for a wide range of elements in Canva, including text, shapes, images, and graphics. You can use transparency to create a variety of effects in your designs, such as making elements appear to blend together, creating a ghosted or faded effect, or adding depth and dimension to your designs.

Trash

The trash is a feature that allows you to delete designs or design elements that you no longer need or want. When you delete a design or element in Canva, it is moved to the trash, where it can be restored or permanently deleted.

To delete a design or element in Canva:
1. Select the design or element that you want to delete.
2. Click the "Delete" button in the toolbar above the canvas.
3. The design or element will be moved to the trash.

To access the trash in Canva:
1. Click on the "Trash" icon in the left-hand bottom toolbar of your dashboard.
2. The trash folder will open, showing a list of all of the designs and elements that have been deleted from your account.

The trash feature in Canva is a useful tool for keeping your account organized and clutter-free. You can use it to restore designs or elements that you want to keep, or permanently delete them. It is important to remember that when an item is deleted from the trash, it cannot be recovered.

🗑 Trash

Trash

Designs   Images   Videos

Typography

Typography involves the use of type (letters, numbers, and symbols) in design. Canva offers a variety of typography tools and features, such as fonts, sizes, colors, spacing, alignment, and effects, to customize the look and feel of text. You can access these tools through the top menu to change the font, size, color, spacing, alignment, and add effects such as drop shadows, glows, and outlines. These tools allow for professional-looking designs that match your brand and style.

Using these typography tools and features, you can create professional-looking designs with customized text that matches your brand and style.

Learn more about typography terms here:
https://www.canva.com/learn/typography-terms/

U

Underline

The "Underline" feature is a text formatting tool that allows you to add an underline to text in a text box. An underline is a horizontal line that is drawn underneath text, and is often used to indicate emphasis or to create a visual hierarchy in a design.

To use the "Underline" feature in Canva:
1. Select the text box that you want to edit.
2. Click on the "Text" tab in the toolbar on the left.
3. Under the "Format" section, click on the "Underline" button

Undo

The "Undo" feature allows you to reverse the effects of the most recent action that you have taken in the editor. This can be useful if you have made a change to your design that you want to undo, or if you want to revert to a previous version of your design.

To use the "Undo" feature in Canva, click on the "Undo" button in the top menu of the editor. This will undo the most recent action that you have taken, such as adding or deleting an element, changing the text or formatting of an element, or moving an element. You can also use the keyboard shortcut "Ctrl+Z" (on Windows) or "Command+Z" (on Mac) to undo an action.

Ungroup

A feature in Canva that allows you to separate elements that have been grouped together into individual elements.

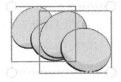

Unique Links

Special URLs known as unique links can be generated to share designs with others and monitor their analytics in the insights feature on the top tool bar. By creating a unique link for a design, it can be shared with anyone, allowing them to view the design in their browser without the need for a Canva account or access to the design itself. This is a convenient way to share designs and track the origin of views and traffic.

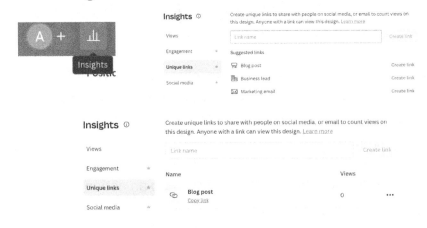

Unlink

A feature in Canva that allows you to separate elements that have been grouped together into individual elements.

Upload

A feature in Canva that allows you to add elements to your design from other sources, such as images or graphics from your computer.

Uppercase

The "Uppercase" feature is a text formatting tool that allows you to convert text to uppercase letters. Uppercase letters are also known as capital letters or majuscules, and are used to write the beginning of a sentence or for emphasis.

To use the "Uppercase" feature in Canva:

- Select the text box that you want to edit.
- Click on the "Text" tab in the toolbar on the left.
- Under the "Format" section, click on the "Uppercase" button.

The "Uppercase" feature in Canva is a quick and easy way to convert text to uppercase letters. It is particularly useful for designers who want to create emphasis or make text stand out in a design.

A B *I* U aA

Uppercase

∙∙

User Interface

The interface of a software program, such as Canva, that allows you to interact with and use the program.

∙∙

US Letter Document

In Canva, a US Letter document refers to a specific page size that is commonly used in the United States. The US Letter size is 8.5 inches wide by 11 inches tall. This size is typically used for a variety of document types such as letterhead, resumes, brochures and many more.

Vector

A type of graphic element that is made up of lines and curves, rather than pixels. Canva allows you to use vector graphics in your designs. Vector files are often used for logos, illustrations, and other graphics that need to be resized frequently without losing quality. A SVG is a type of vector file, but not all vector files are SVG files.

■■■

Version History

In Canva, version history is a feature that allows users to view and restore previous versions of a design. When you save a design in Canva, a new version of the design is created and added to the version history. This allows you to go back and view previous versions of the design and compare them to the current version.

To access the version history of a design in Canva, click on the "File" menu and select "Version history" from the dropdown menu. This will open a window that displays a list of all the versions of the design, with the most recent version at the top. You can click on any version in the list to view it, or you can use the "Restore" button to restore a previous version of the design as the current version.

Version history can be a useful tool for tracking changes to a design and for undoing mistakes or changes that you don't want to keep. It is especially useful when working on a design with a team, as it allows you to see what changes have been made by different team members.

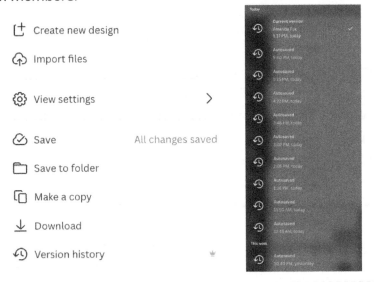

Vertical

A direction in Canva that is perpendicular to the horizontal direction, running from top to bottom. You can "flip" an image or graphic using the flip button and change the position.

Video

A feature in Canva that allows you to add a video to your design, either by uploading a video file or by linking to a video online.

You can upload videos using the "uploads" tab in the left-hand vertical toolbar, or add videos using the "embed" feature in the "apps section. You can find previously uploaded videos in the "uploads" tab by selecting videos.

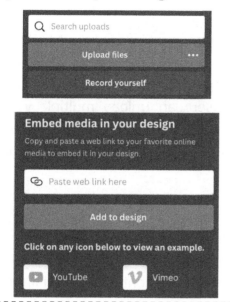

Video Background Remover

Video Background remover in Canva is similar to the image background remover. When you add a video to your design you can remove that background of that video in one click. This works best in videos that have a solid background.

Video background remover is limited to videos under 90 seconds.

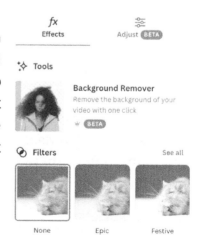

Video Collage

A video collage in Canva is a feature that allows you to combine multiple videos into a single video collage. This feature allows users to create a dynamic and engaging visual experience by combining multiple videos into one. The user can upload multiple videos, resize, and reposition the videos on a single canvas and add texts, shapes, and other design elements to create a unique and creative visual.

The video collage can be exported as a video file, which can be shared on various platforms like social media, websites, and more. Video collages are great for creating promotional videos, storytelling, and creating dynamic visual content for social media and marketing campaigns.

Read more here:
https://www.canva.com/create/video-collages/

Video Message

A video message template in Canva is a customized video to celebrate or acknowledge a milestone, event, or holiday. By customizing one of these video message templates, you can give the celebrant a greeting that they will treasure forever.

See Video Message templates here:
https://www.canva.com/video-messages/templates/

Video Transitions

Video transitions can be added between your slides for nice visual effect between videos. To add transitions between video clips or slides, click the + icon located between each one. Select "Add Transition" from the menu, and the Transitions sidebar will appear. Choose a transition, and click on its icon to set its duration and direction.

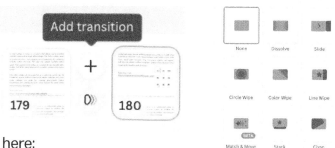

Read more here:
https://www.canva.com/features/video-transitions/

Video Trimmer

The "Video Trimmer" in Canva is a feature that allows you to cut and remove unwanted sections from the beginning or end of a video. To use it, select the video in your design and use the "Video Trimmer" window to set the start and end points by dragging the sliders or entering specific times. Preview the trimmed video using the "Play" button and make any final adjustments. Click "Trim Video" to save changes. This feature can help you edit and refine your videos, making them shorter and more focused for easier sharing and consumption.

Read more here:
https://www.canva.com/help/trim-videos/

■■

View as List

"View as List" is a feature in Canva that allows you to view your designs as a list rather than as thumbnails. This feature is useful for quickly finding specific designs or for organizing your designs in a more efficient way.

To use the "View as List" feature in Canva:
1. Open the "My Designs" tab in the Canva editor.
2. Click on the "View as List" button in the top right corner of the "My Designs" tab.
3. The designs will be displayed as a list rather than as thumbnails.
4.

The "View as List" feature in Canva is a useful tool for quickly finding specific designs or for organizing your designs in a more efficient way. It can be particularly useful for designers who have a large number of designs in their Canva account and who want to be able to easily find specific designs. You can also see who has access to the design and who it has been shared with.

View Only Link

To share a design without allowing viewers to make edits or copy your design in Canva, go to the "Share" tab in the top right corner of the editor and click on "View Only Link". This will generate a unique URL that can be shared with others to view the design, but not make any changes or download/print without permission. This is useful for getting feedback or sharing with clients/stakeholders who only need to view the design.

Read more about sharing links here:
https://www.canva.com/help/share-via-link-or-email/

Vision Simulator

An app filter created by Adee that allows users to apply a color-blind filter to designs so designers can view work from the perspective of someone that is color-blind.

Read more about the app here:
https://www.canva.com/your-apps/AAEthvh1gvl-vision-simulator

W

Wallpaper

A template maker in Canva that allows users to customize wallpapers for your desktop. You can also create wallpapers for your phone. See "phone wallpaper."

Read more here:
https://www.canva.com/create/wallpapers/

Webpage/Website

Canva website builder lets users quickly build and design functional and interactive website that are great for product launches, classroom websites, bio websites, e-commerce, businesses, and more! With it's drag and drop user interface it's easy to build a website from scratch or use one of their pre-designed templates to get up and running.

You can preview your website and publish it to the web. You can use a Canva domain, or link a domain you have purchased.

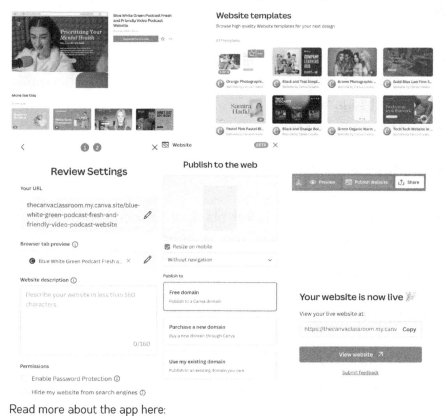

Read more about the app here:
https://www.canva.com/website-builder/

Web-safe font

A font that is widely available on the internet and is likely to be installed on most computers, ensuring that text in your design will be displayed correctly on the web. Canva offers a selection of web-safe fonts.

Read this blog on Web-safe fonts:
https://www.canva.com/learn/web-fonts/

••

Width

The distance between the left and right sides of an element, such as an image or graphic. Canva allows you to adjust the width of elements in your designs.

••

White Space

The area in a design that is left blank or unoccupied by elements. Canva allows you to adjust the amount of white space in your designs to create a balanced layout.

••

Whiteboard

Canva's Whiteboard templates are interactive, digital workspaces that enable virtual collaboration with teams or classes. They are ideal for collecting ideas, brainstorming, and organizing tasks and projects with a team.

To use the Whiteboard Feature:

Search for "whiteboard" on your Canva account and select your favorite template or create one from scratch.

Use the share menu to invite your team members and begin collaborating on the whiteboard template. Utilize real-time mouse pointers, a timer and commenting and reaction features to enhance the collaboration process. The template also includes a variety of tools such as stickies, graphics, line connectors, flow charts and more to help you and your team visually organize and present ideas.

After your whiteboard session, you can easily use other Canva tools like presentations or share to social media and bring your project to life.

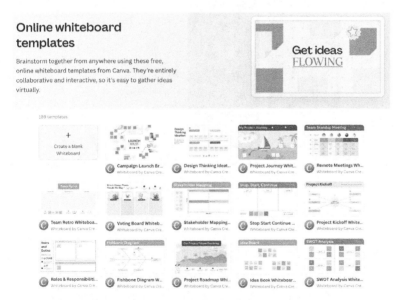

Check out these Canva whiteboard templates:
https://www.canva.com/online-whiteboard/templates/

Wireframe

A simple, basic layout of a webpage or application, used to plan the structure and functionality of a design. In Canva, you can find a number of wire frame templates to create prototypes and mockups for apps. This is great for testing the user interface and sharing basic drag-and-drop builds to share with clients and developers.

Workflow

The process of creating and managing designs in Canva, including creating new designs, editing and customizing elements, and collaborating with others. Canva has so many integrated native apps that just using the platform will reduce your workflow and save you time.

Worksheet

In Canva, worksheet templates are pre-designed and customizable templates for creating various types of worksheets, such as educational, budget, planner, and more. These templates can be used to create worksheets for different purposes like, for example, educational worksheets for students, budget worksheets for personal finance, planner worksheets for scheduling and organizing tasks. They are available in a variety of formats and designs, and can be easily edited and customized to meet the needs of the user. They can be used for personal, educational or professional use.

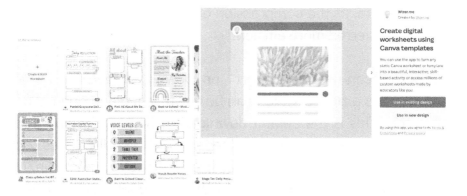

Check out worksheet templates here:
https://www.canva.com/worksheets/templates/

Furthermore, you can use the Wizer app connection to export your worksheets for auto-grading features.

Read more about Wizer Worksheets here:
https://www.canva.com/learn/canva-and-wizer-make-worksheets-interactive-and-engaging/

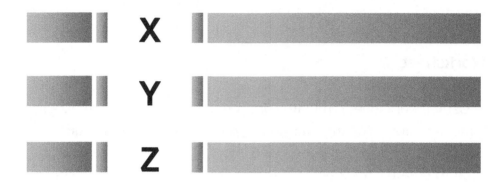

Zip File

A zip file in Canva is a compressed archive file that contains multiple files or folders that have been bundled together into a single file. Zip files are often used to store and transfer large amounts of data, as the compression of the files allows them to be stored or transferred more efficiently.

In Canva, you can use the "Export" or "Download" feature to save your designs as a zip file, which can be downloaded and opened on a computer. This is the default download setting for designs that have multiple pages and are downloaded as PNG or JPEG files. Zip files can be opened using a file decompression tool, such as WinZip or 7-Zip, which allows you to extract the individual files or folders contained in the zip file.

Zoom

In Canva, the zoom feature allows you to increase or decrease the magnification of your design. You can zoom in to work on specific details or zoom out to view the overall layout of your design. This can be useful when you want to make precise adjustments to your design, or when you want to see how your design looks at different sizes. The zoom feature can be accessed by using the zoom slider in the bottom right corner of the Canva editor, or by using keyboard shortcuts like "Ctrl +" to zoom in and "Ctrl -" to zoom out on a PC, or "Command +" and "Command -" on a Mac. Additionally, you can also use the zoom tool from the toolbar to click and drag over an area of the design that you want to zoom in on.

125% ⬤

Zoom Virtual Background

In Canva, you can use the Zoom Virtual backgrounds feature to create custom backgrounds for your Zoom calls. They have a variety of templates and design elements that can be used to create a background that fits the theme or tone of your call. Once you have designed your background, you can upload it to Zoom and select it as your virtual background during your call.

Read more about zoom backgrounds here:
https://www.canva.com/create/zoom-virtual-background/

# About the Author

Amanda Fox is an award winning teacher and Savannah, Georgia native who currently lives and works in Prospect, Kentucky. She is the Chief Content Officer for TeacherGoals. Recipient of the 2016 ISTE Emerging Leader Award, recognized as a PBS Digital innovator for her initiatives in enhancing student learning with technology, Fox has also served as President of the Young Educator Network for ISTE, and received the President's Volunteer Award.

She is author of The Hitchhiker's Guide to the Canva Classroom, Teachingland, Zom-Be a Design Thinker, and the Markertown Series. Her inspiration for Markertown came from her kids Rowan, Bridgit, Connor, and Finn, who are constantly giving her ideas for new stories and adventures to inspire the world. She believes caps should always be put back on markers, and toothpaste, but never Mexican cokes. Learn more or connect with Amanda on Twitter @AmandaFoxSTEM or via email at amanda@teachergoals.com.

For more information on booking Amanda for book readings, summer camps, keynotes, workshops, design thinking led sessions, or video conferencing/virtual book readings with your class or school, go to teachergoals.com/pd.

For awesome classroom content and activities for Markertown, check out teachergoals.com/markertown!

Cultivate Canva Classrooms in Your District

#THECANVACLASSROOM WORKSHOP

How can you leverage Canva to its fullest potential to cultivate the 4 C's in your district, while also saving time, but not sacrificing rigor? With Canva, lessons can be pretty AND powerful! In this session or workshop Amanda will share classroom tested templates and strategies and unlock hidden tips to boost not only teacher engagement, but also student outcomes. Reach out to contact@teachergoals.com to book Amanda for a transformative professional development experience that will have everyone believing they can, can, can.

#THECANVACLASSROOM KEYNOTE

In this fun and engaging keynote, chocked full of pop culture references, educators are invited to hitchhike their way through a beautifully designed universe of templates that span all content and grade levels. Built on the foundation of DOK, UDL, and UBD teachers will walk away inspired and grounded in good pedagogy. Amanda will share her educational journey and the dreams for what education could and should be.

For more information on professional development go to www.teachergoals.com/pd.

Made in the USA
Middletown, DE
26 July 2023

35762876R00113